ALSO BY THE AUTHORS

The Magic of Tarot
Catalog of the Unexplained
Fairy Soap

LEANNA GREENAWAY

The Holistic Witch (with Shawn Robbins)
Psychic Spellcraft (with Shawn Robbins)
Wiccapedia Spell Deck (with Shawn Robbins)
The Crystal Witch (with Shawn Robbins)
The Witch's Way (with Shawn Robbins)
Wiccapedia Journal (with Shawn Robbins)
Tarot Plain and Simple
Wicca Plain and Simple
Practical Spellcraft
Wiccapedia (with Shawn Robbins)

BELETA GREENAWAY

The Little Book of Meditation
The Little Book of Crystals
*Out of Your Hands: What Palmistry Reveals About Your Personality
and Destiny*
Angels Plain and Simple

"There are times we have negative thoughts and feelings toward others and others have them toward us. This book is incredibly important as it demonstrates why they are harmful and how to best protect ourselves and others with simple yet powerful methods. Release fear and get empowered with this essential tool kit, especially valuable for highly sensitive people."

—KRIS FERRARO, international energy healer, speaker, and author of *Manifesting, Your Difference Is Your Strength,* and *Energy Healing*

"In *The Book of Psychic Self-Defense,* you'll find a plethora of techniques and tools you can use to chase away intrusive nonphysical entities and protect yourself from psychic attack. . . . Whatever your reason for digging into the subject, you'll gain information, insight, and practical guidance from this fascinating book."

—SKYE ALEXANDER, author of *The Modern Guide to Witchcraft* and *The Modern Witchcraft Spell Book*

"The award-winning mother-daughter team Beleta and Leanna Greenaway have coauthored yet another book that is as insightful as it is helpful. These two Devon-based wise women have over four decades of experience in working with and investigating the world of the psychic, the esoteric, and, in this case, the downright evil. They have drawn on this experience to produce a comprehensive and skillfully written guide for those seeking protection from energetic and supernatural attacks. There is an emphasis on practical methods of self-protection that include rituals, some involving chants and simple props, which can be done at home for ease and privacy. . . . The authors' compassion shines through—their wish to not only inform but to help others through practical advice and down-to-earth solutions; their dedication to ensuring that love and light overcome harm from dark forces."

—ANNA MCKENNA, author of *The Little Book of Astrology* and lecturer in English as a foreign language at the University of Plymouth

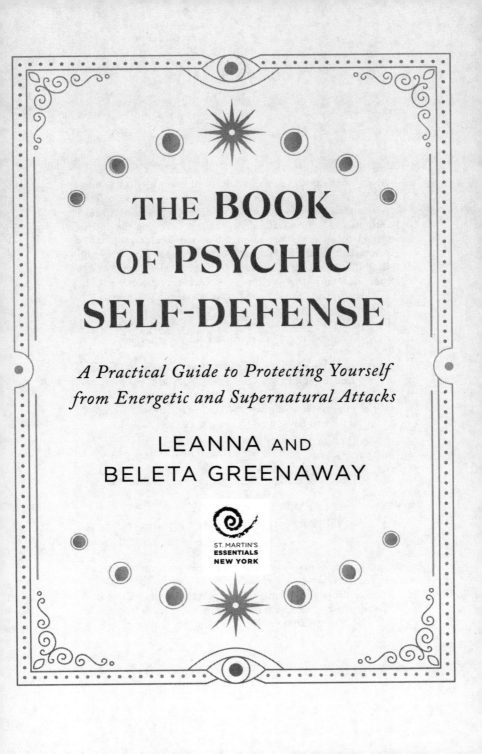

THE **BOOK**
OF **PSYCHIC**
SELF-DEFENSE

*A Practical Guide to Protecting Yourself
from Energetic and Supernatural Attacks*

LEANNA AND
BELETA GREENAWAY

ST. MARTIN'S
ESSENTIALS
NEW YORK

First published in the United States by St. Martin's Essentials, an imprint of St. Martin's Publishing Group

THE BOOK OF PSYCHIC SELF-DEFENSE. Copyright © 2024 by Leanna and Beleta Greenaway. All rights reserved. Printed in the United States of America. For information, address St. Martin's Publishing Group, 120 Broadway, New York, NY 10271.

www.stmartins.com

The Library of Congress Cataloging-in-Publication Data is available upon request.

ISBN 978-1-250-32390-3 (trade paperback)
ISBN 978-1-250-32391-0 (ebook)

Our books may be purchased in bulk for promotional, educational, or business use. Please contact your local bookseller or the Macmillan Corporate and Premium Sales Department at 1-800-221-7945, extension 5442, or by email at MacmillanSpecialMarkets@macmillan.com.

First Edition: 2024

10 9 8 7 6 5 4 3 2 1

*This book is dedicated to all the kind people
who gave their permission for us to use their case studies.
We understand that recalling these terrifying events
was difficult for you at the time, but we hope that
your stories will comfort our readers in some way
in the future.*

CONTENTS

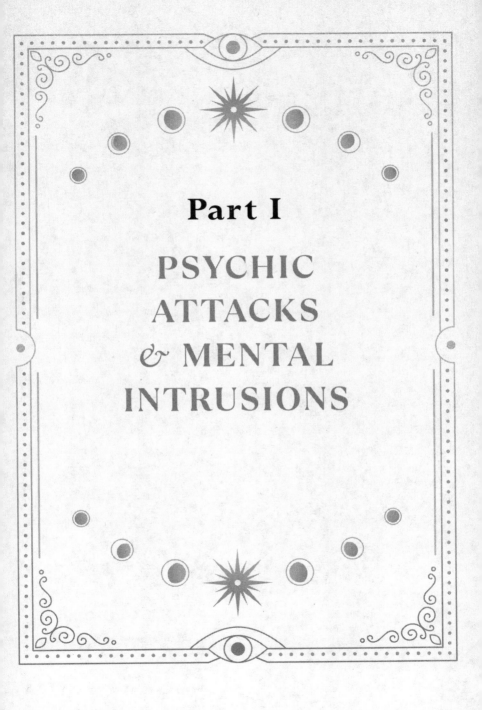

Part I

PSYCHIC ATTACKS & MENTAL INTRUSIONS

A PROJECTED THOUGHT OR A person's mindset carries energy, and when something negative is propelled into the world, be it an idea, an action, a spoken word, or a spell, the vibration is usually transmitted directly to the intended person. There are so many ways an individual can fall victim to psychic assault, and any one of us can deliberately or unintentionally cast a dark cloud over someone. Energy may be invisible, but it's everywhere, and everyone taps into it daily. Have you ever walked into a party of people where the assembly is jovial and cheerful? The music may be uplifting, and everyone is chattering and having a great time, so the positive energy in the room will instantly lift one's mood. The same can be said if we join a group of people who are laughing hysterically; even though we didn't hear the joke, we will automatically begin to giggle. If you are unfortunate enough to live with someone who is depressed, you are likely to be impacted by their unhappiness, or if you sit at the back of a church when a funeral is in process, you will instinctively pick up on the grief and suffering of the congregation. These are classic examples of how we receive infectious energy without even realizing it.

You've heard the expression "You could cut the atmosphere with a knife." Let's say there have been arguments and rows in a home, which may have taken place over a few weeks; the vibrations inside the house will feel oppressive, so any outsider entering the property could get an unsettling feeling. We generate energy every moment we're alive, and the human soul is extremely sensitive to it.

THE COLLECTIVE CONSCIOUSNESS

Also known as hive mind, group mind, mass mind

WHEN A GROUP OF PEOPLE, be it large or small, spiritual or not, harmonize their thoughts and beliefs, it is said to strengthen their ability to influence events. For example, when we manifest energy, imagine a gathering of people focusing on one specific goal. The energy generated will be amplified to such an extent and cause the desire to materialize; this is how spells and rituals are performed and how religious prayers spoken en masse may bring about a change in some way.

Positive collective consciousness is widely believed to elevate the soul to a higher vibration. Still, negative collective consciousness is supercharged and significantly impacts the matrix, holding back the potential of a united Earth.

When a country at war contaminates the social structures of other peaceful nations, it can cause adverse karma that can spread at an alarming rate. Eventually, this insufferable energy of the world's people will cast a negative ball of dark mass toward the tormentor. For instance, when the media broadcasts horrible images of animal and human abuse into our homes, it sends shockwaves throughout the entire world, affecting millions of individuals. The despair and misery the masses feel then fuel undesirable thoughts, which generate bad energy. When these negative vibes reach the wrongdoers, they can become ill, suffer misfortune in their private lives, and even undergo mental anguish. Thought projection is a genuine and often dangerous factor; therefore, the shared consciousness must be amalgamated to balance out any evil to restore harmony.

THE EVIL EYE

A thought is a living thing.

THE EVIL EYE IS A curse that dates back more than five thousand years. It's described as a malicious stare that is said to bring bad luck, material loss, illness, and, at worst, death. It has become ubiquitous in many religions, such as Islam, Buddhism, Hinduism, and Judaism, and throughout the world, numerous folk societies hold this belief, too. It begins when someone stares at the victim with evil intent, silently wishing or verbalizing that something terrible will happen to them. An interesting experiment shows that if someone stares intently at the back of a person's head, say, at a party or gathering, the victim might instinctively sense they are under scrutiny and look around to see why they feel so uncomfortable. This "death stare" can also be used on unsuspecting animals; horses are one species that is particularly sensitive to this. Another way to cast the evil eye is to stand and point at an individual while at the same time telling them you wish them bad luck. Sometimes, the evil eye can be carried out in private, and the recipient will be completely unaware of what is happening.

Most individuals are oblivious to how their mindset can impact others. Understanding the brain's potential can empower an individual to take charge of their body and subconsciously change the energy they emit.

Today, psychic people suppose that even a negative, flippant remark can manifest into a black cloud of energy. Like the collective consciousness, it begins with a harmful thought directed toward a particular individual or enemy. This form of mind power is so subtle; as mentioned above, the targeted individual is often unaware that anything untoward is happening. It is also the case that even if we detest someone, for whatever reason, the energy we muster can propel a barrage of ill fortune toward them. One example might be a vindictive mother-in-law who despises her son's wife. She may criticize or complain about her privately or to anyone who will listen or blatantly to the daughter-in-law herself. Silent loathing can also create an evil eye, so it's not necessarily true that the perpetrator must verbalize a dislike for someone. It doesn't matter how we choose to do it; whether we are aware we are doing it or oblivious to it, we are still conjuring negative energy.

It is common for recently divorced individuals going through acrimonious breakups with ex-partners to experience this. The couple have probably been unhappy for months preceding the split, and then situations such as romantic affairs, non-payment of child support, or custody battles occur. One partner or both may reach the stage where they loath the other, and so, unintentionally, the evil eye will be cast. Suddenly, their life might spiral out of control; they could lose their job, suffer financial loss, or even become sick.

CASE STUDY: BELETA
POWERFUL WORDS

When my husband and I were newly married, we had saved long and hard to purchase our first home. It was an end-of-terrace new property on the brow of a hill, and although it wasn't much, it was ours. Shortly after moving in, it became clear that the lady next door despised our cats and could be heard shouting at them when they entered her garden. Knowing how cats roam and, at times, how they dig up other people's gardens, we did understand that only some are as passionate about the feline species as we are. Still, it is challenging to contain cats or monitor where they go, primarily when they are used to their freedom. She would regularly knock on my door to complain, and after a while, my patience wore thin, and so eventually, our dislike for each other became very apparent.

One morning, my husband, John, was assembling a cat run in the garden while Leanna and I were washing the dishes in the kitchen. My neighbor walked past our window and was headed toward her car when she turned toward me and childishly stuck out her tongue. Without thinking, I whispered under my breath, "Oh, I hope your car breaks down." Suddenly, as she opened the driver's door, the vehicle began to roll down the hill. She immediately ran after it but couldn't keep up; the car eventually crashed into someone's front porch. Leanna stood beside me aghast and said, "Mother, what did you just do!" Of course, it could have been purely coincidental, but perhaps it wasn't! I was so enraged by this woman that I directed all my hatred and anger toward her. Thankfully no one was hurt!

Another example of the evil eye occurred many years ago when a friend was annoyed with her caged canary. The bird was being boisterous and was making a lot of noise, and in a moment of frustration, she turned to the bird and spat out, "I wish you'd just drop dead." The canary fell off its perch and immediately passed away.

CASE STUDY: JANE
THE AWFUL BOSS

When I was in my early twenties, my dad interviewed for a high-flying company that offered a brand-new car, private health care, an excellent pension, and a great wage. Fifteen people had applied for the job, so you can imagine how proud the family was when he landed such a prestigious position. All was good initially; he had a female boss, liked the staff, and was doing exceptionally well. After a few months, he started to comment about how rude his boss was becoming and how she always talked down to him. He was the top salesman in the company and was praised by other senior managers, so we could only suppose she was jealous of his success. Over the next few months, her behavior worsened. She would give him impossible tasks, raise his target to something unrealistic, and increase his workload, so he naturally fell behind. The final straw came when she deliberately criticized him in front of his team members, calling him worthless. This woman was a straight-up bully. He had even gone to one of the company's senior members to see if anything could be done, but back then, people did very little to help. One evening he came home from work, and my lovely, strong, dependable dad was crumbling. I could see his confidence diminishing; he looked strained and tearful, and Mother and I felt powerless to help. In a fit of rage, I shouted out in anger, "I hope the bitch falls down and breaks her neck!" I'm not proud of what I said, but it was a knee-jerk reaction to seeing my dad so vulnerable at the time.

The following day, he came home from work, and I knew something was wrong when I saw the look on his face. He quietly told me his boss had fallen over at work and broken her collarbone.

To ensure you're not accidentally jinxing anyone, it's best to keep one's thoughts as pure as possible, and if you feel anger rising inside you, try hard to remain neutral; this is much easier said than done, especially if someone has done something hurtful or unkind. Most of us are fiercely protective of those we love, so should they come up against anyone who mistreats them, our emotions stir from deep within, and we immediately go into defense mode.

Of course, our friend didn't want her canary to die, and neither of us would have wanted to cause a potentially fatal accident with a car and a porch. Jane certainly felt responsible when her father's boss had her accident. Still, it begs the question, if it is so easy to channel negative energy and unintentionally cause someone harm, what happens if someone deliberately sends the evil eye?

In all four corners of the world, there are those who practice dark magic and enjoy targeting their victims with the evil eye. They will go out of their way to psychically attack their enemies and sometimes extend the curse to the victim's family members.

CAUSE AND EFFECT

BEARING IN MIND THAT ALL thoughts are living things and that evil is attracted to malevolent intentions, we should always be conscious of our words and actions.

Many people will casually use profanities in daily life, such as swearing at a driver who cut them off in the road or using a vulgar gesture to express their anger.

In truth, this is a form of cursing and in that moment they are venting their negative energy toward another person, which then attaches itself to the receiver's aura. Similarly, if someone is talking to a person and keeps pointing at them rudely, it's akin to using a witch's gesture. An example would be pointing a wand and summoning its power to create a spell. All thoughts and deeds have a cause and effect, so when we flippantly cast out these actions, we can harm someone unintentionally.

SIGNS YOU MAY BE UNDER PSYCHIC ATTACK

- Feeling tired all the time or even exhausted without any medical explanation
- Frequent nightmares or bouts of sleep paralysis
- Sporadic bouts of insomnia
- A lengthy period of bad luck or feeling as though you are stuck in glue
- Suffering from spells of depression or being low or tearful without explanation

- Wondering whether you are losing your mind or questioning your sanity
- Experiencing minor ailments that keep reoccurring after a period of being well, including colds, flu-like symptoms, or difficulty breathing (if you have an underlying health problem, this will surface more often)
- Feeling colder than usual or never being able to get warm
- Becoming snappy or showing more aggressive behavior
- Sensing you are cursed
- Experiencing strange skin sensations, like insects crawling over all parts of your body
- Having suicidal thoughts or wondering how people would react if you died
- Pets becoming sick or dying

Many disbelieve this theory, but it happens to thousands of people every minute of the day. The more enemies you accumulate in life, the more likely you will experience some form of attack if you don't protect yourself adequately.

Of course, if you are experiencing any of the above, it's not strictly true that you are being targeted with the evil eye. There are always alternative explanations, such as illness or other underlying health conditions. You may be just having a run of bad luck, which happens to everyone at some point in their life. However, if you are convinced that someone is psychically attacking you, first, you have to think long and hard about any enemies you have or those you may have treated poorly at some stage in your life. Even if you picked on a kid in fourth grade or were unkind to someone without it being deserved, many people who have been mistreated hang on to these negative emotions for years and even decades, so even though their psychic attack is unintentional or sent by accident, you need to know what you are up against.

INVOLUNTARY FORMS
OF EVIL INTENT

BULLYING

MANY WOULD CONSIDER PULLING PRACTICAL jokes or making fun of others to be harmless, but even though an action might be done without malice, if it's not well received, it creates a damaging energy field around the target, which causes unhappiness and sometimes depression. This negative energy could develop a perpetual dark cloud around them that may lower their spiritual vibration. Often, a mass of depressive buildup is an open invitation for any sinister entity to attach itself, feeding off its negative energy field.

Unintentional bullying can also occur in large families, where one member might differ from the rest of the clan. It happens in the wild: If one animal is smaller or different from the others, the rest of the pack will attack them; this can also happen with humans. The main players in the family see the odd one out as a threat and will round up on them, putting them down all the time and making them know their place. Often a more evolved soul will reincarnate into a family of lower vibrational souls to help teach them new things. However, the family will look down on the victim's opinions or not allow them a voice, gradually chipping away at their self-confidence. In situations like these, the negative collective consciousness of the clan gathers power, and the victim is sometimes driven out to find their own life. Even if they are far away from the family, any ill thoughts or negative gossip can manifest ill will that will be directed to the individual. If someone feels they are the victim of this situation, they must remain strong and stand up for their principles.

TROLLING

YOUNGER AGE groups are currently dealing with challenges that previous generations have not faced. Believe it or not, trolling is also a way of casting an evil eye on someone. Pen and paper magic is a typical practice in witchcraft for manifesting goals or intentions, and even though we often type these days instead of writing by hand, it still produces comparable energy. What gives trolling more clout is that the magical malpractice has an audience, and hundreds, if not millions, of young people (often like-minded) can provide momentum to the curse. Spiteful words and heckling can cause harmful energy, even to the point the victim considers suicide. One might wonder if the perpetrators are motivated by darker forces and compelled to make others' lives unbearable. There is usually a reason why someone takes pleasure in victimizing others. If this behavior continues into adulthood, it is more likely they are a lower vibrational soul who might, upon death, evolve into an evil spirit. Often, it is just a case of a bully being unhappy themselves, and so with no way of knowing how to channel that anger, they inflict their misery on others.

SOLUTION

WHEN A young person is targeted by trolls, they must come off social media altogether for a while so that the negative energy doesn't have a direct path to their door. Any parent or guardian needs to ensure that the troll has no access to their child whatsoever, so they must block them on cell phones, emails, and other ways of communication. Of course, we know the evil eye doesn't always need a platform to work. Usually, if an adult faces malicious intent, there are ways to protect themselves with rituals or spells that magically send the curse back to its source. Still, this isn't wise in the case of youngsters, as there is usually a reason for behaving in such a manner. Often, children who target others are reacting to negative situations in their life. Perhaps their home life is spiraling out of control or they are being mistreated by a parent or sibling.

To protect your child, they need to be empowered with lots of positive energy, support, and words of encouragement. Try to explain that the bully is doing it for a reaction, and the best thing they can do is not engage. It would help if you threw everything you could at combating this problem, and depending on how badly the youngster is affected by the trolling, you might have to spend a great deal of time talking things through with them. Therapy is also advised.

Another way to protect the young person from further trolling or bullying is to place the child in the center of a salt circle. Salt is renowned for its protective properties and will act as a barrier to all negative vibes. The collective consciousness is all-powerful, so every member of the family, young and old, must stand around the salt circle, holding one another's hands. Together recite the following mantra twelve times:

"We stand together and protect you; nothing can hinder you; nothing can harm you."

This will manifest light around the youngster and defer negative energy away.

CASE STUDY: JEANETTE STALKING

An old friend we hadn't heard from in a long time called us one day and immediately burst into tears. She was in her eighties, and we could hear the fear in her voice. After she had calmed down, she told us she had been terrorized for two years by an unseen man who would prowl around outside her bungalow in the small hours. He would bang on every window while she crouched in the darkness. Sometimes gravel was thrown at the glass, and often he would ring her doorbell. Jeanette is a gentle spinster who had told no one of her ordeal. Contacting us was a cry for help, and we immediately jumped into action. We used spell craft and summoned the angels to protect her. Being in our line of work we are blessed to have many healers around us, so we approached them on Facebook. They all sent absent healing, directing positive prayers for her protection. We thought it was a good idea for her to connect with the minister and congregation of her local church for added support, and they, too, said their prayers and blessings. We also encouraged her to knock on her neighbors' doors to let them know this sinister man was stalking her. Even the police played their part and installed cameras and security lights around her property.

The love and sympathy sent to her was remarkable, and she started to feel more confident and optimistic. After a few weeks of everyone's support, she phoned to thank us and said she hadn't seen the man since.

Although this wasn't a psychic attack, it was psychological, and the methods for dealing with a situation like this are exactly the same.

Facebook is a fantastic tool for harnessing the power of the human consciousness. Often, when so many people send out thoughts and prayers for someone's safety, it can profoundly affect and encircle the victim in a positive light. We often use social media to tap into the collective consciousness if someone is sick or needs healing, and nine times out of ten, the energy they manifest through their love and sympathy can cure or speed up the healing process.

PROTECTING YOURSELF

The main creative powers in your life are your thoughts.

ONE OF THE QUICKEST AND most effective ways of combating the evil eye or any other form of psychic attack perpetrated by a living person is to find the source. First, look toward those in your social circle. Have you upset somebody? Is someone jealous of you? Perhaps you said something to a neighbor or friend and hurt their feelings. Be blatantly honest with yourself, and even if you had an upset with someone and you believe you were right, try to put yourself in their position for a moment and understand their point of view. It's important to try to make amends and offer an apology. Your main aim is to change the other person's mindset, and you will only be able to achieve this if you are no longer the aggressor. Sometimes, just a few words of kindness can diffuse any bad situation, so facing the issue head-on and admitting any mistakes you might have made is an excellent way to undo the curse. If this doesn't work and your enemy is unwilling to wipe the slate clean, you need to manifest positive energy around yourself so that the negative vibes cannot reach you. Focus on the good things in your life, and by lightening the vibration, you can remove a marker that might attract unpleasant attention.

If you feel you are cursed with the evil eye but have no idea who has sent this to you, a more practical approach is needed. Carrying amulets and talismans can sometimes be enough to stop the curse in its tracks.

THE MELONG MIRROR

THE MELONG mirror is a popular amulet for shamanic, Mongolian, and Tibetan practices and is often worn to adorn their costumes. Multiple mirrors are sometimes sewn onto garments around the torso area to form a protective shield repelling the evil eye.

In Tibet, mirrors are often used to help people see the nature of their karma. By gazing into it, the past, present, and future can reveal themselves, providing the opportunity to see one's spiritual itinerary and to guard against any negative psychic attacks. Large Melong mirrors are often suspended outside doorways to chase away anything menacing and prevent unwanted vibrations from entering a person's home. In today's society, the mirrors can be smaller, made of copper or brass, and worn as amulets around the neck; this is also extra helpful for nighttime protection. These can be purchased inexpensively online and, when worn, will reflect all evil intentions away from you.

MORE MIRROR PROTECTION

BUYING SOME little mosaic mirrors is another powerful approach to repel the evil eye. These can be purchased relatively cheaply online or in craft shops. For every window in your house, you will need one little mirror. If there are many windowpanes, treat them as one. First, to empower the mirrors with your desire, set them all out with the mirror facing upward on a flat surface. Light a white tealight candle somewhere beside them and silently concentrate on your intention. Tell the mirrors their purpose and how you want them to serve you. Something like:

> *"I need your protection. Send negativity away. Shield me from the evil eye."*

We've established that we can influence energy with our intent, but we can also add power to the ritual by using our breath. Pick up one of the mirrors, hold it for about thirty seconds, and stare into the reflective surface. Imagine any negative vibes bouncing straight off the mirror. While doing this, take deep breaths in, and then breathe out your positive energy onto the surface. Repeat this with each mirror.

Once you have completed this, you can blow out the candle. Rest one mirror facing outward in the corner of every window of your home. Any bad vibes sent your way will immediately be returned to the sender.

Whether you believe you are being affected by the evil eye or not, it's good practice to use the mirrors this way as they will always protect the home and its occupants.

THE NAZAR

THE NAZAR, well-known in Greek society, is a cobalt blue amulet made of glass with an eye in the center. Its job is to ward off *maljo*, "bad eye," and keep its owner safe from the dark forces. Some say if a curse is sent, this amulet is powerful enough to direct it back to the perpetrator. It also summons the spirits of calmness and brings karmic protection with its vibrations of defense. It is said to be so powerful it can annihilate the curse instantly.

⚜ USING LIMES AND CLOVES ⚜

Any citrus fruit is renowned for having protective properties, but limes are said to trump them all when used to counterattack the evil eye.

You will need:
1 lime
4 cloves
7 garlic cloves, peeled
White vinegar

Cut the lime into four pieces, then press one clove into the flesh of each section. Put the limes in a glass and add the seven garlic cloves. Pour enough vinegar until everything in the glass is covered. Leave it in the corner of your bedroom for a week to break the curse. After the week has come to an end, empty the contents into the trash and wash the glass with hot water and soap.

❋ USING GARLIC ❋

This garlic ritual should only be carried out if you have exhausted all other avenues, as it will propel any negative energy back to the source and can cause chaos for its creator. Witches are known for using garlic to remove hexes, and most are responsible when doing so. Try not to add any more bad energy to the curse and keep your thoughts neutral.

You will need:
Large plate
White vinegar
1 clove garlic
Piece of paper
Pen with red ink
Scissors

Pour the vinegar onto the plate and submerge the paper in the vinegar so it is adequately coated. Finely chop the clove of garlic and sprinkle this on top. After a few seconds, remove the paper and leave it somewhere to dry thoroughly.

When the paper is dry, use the red pen to write your name on it with the words:
"Cast out the evil eye—RETURN TO SENDER."

Cut the paper into tiny pieces with the scissors while reciting this mantra:

"You will not take my power; I banish you this hour.
My shield cannot break; with this hex that you make,
Ill fortune you'll find in all that you do.
When the evil eye is sent back to you."

AURIC FIELD PROTECTION

THE AURIC field has its roots in Eastern philosophy and is a pulsating vibrational energy that emanates from all human beings. It is said to span up to twenty-five feet of the chakra's vibrations and has a combined explosion of rainbow hues emanating from them. One's auric field may change depending on the surroundings or moods of the individual. Still, with practice, a person can cultivate the strength of their aura and implement it as an energetic boundary to ward off psychic attacks. It's best to remember that we are responsible for what is allowed in and out of our auric field, so great care must be taken to think only positive thoughts.

Each night before you go to sleep, visualize your aura pulsating with positive energy. In your mind, repeat this mantra over and over until you drift off to sleep:

"As positive energy flows through my being, I deflect any negative vibes."

MIND POWER

BECAUSE EVERY thought we send out potentially comes back to us, our desires can be all-powerful. Even if we unintentionally direct our feelings toward a much-wanted outcome, we generate energy within our core that can be set free; this can occur when we constantly imagine how a situation might play out or if we are inadvertently obsessing over something. Our thoughts can be guided toward any specific goal, good or bad. If you genuinely believe your actions can lead to success, they will, but if you concentrate only on your fears and dread, you risk setting yourself up for failure. Many people practice the art of positive mind power manifestation, making their ideas come to life by applying these concepts. If this is the first time you've done something like this, it can take a few attempts to get it right. Suppose a protection ritual is to be successful. In that case, you must summon every ounce of positive energy within yourself and truly believe, without any doubt, that your actions will bring the desired results. Any uncertainty or disbelief could thwart the process. It may take some practice, but once you've perfected the technique, you can cast out any negativity and regain control of your life.

MIND POWER MANTRA

TAKE A seat in front of a mirror and examine your face closely. Say something like:

"I surround myself in a positive light; I have an invisible barrier around me. There is nothing that can harm me within my space. I am protected by the light, and I feel secure."

When you repeat a mantra like this, the energy surrounding you will naturally shift from negative to positive. Regularly carry out the process throughout the day or when you pass a mirror. It will serve as a reflecting medium and will send whatever you wish back to you. Your mood will improve, and you'll experience a sense of peace.

CASE STUDY: BELETA
SUMMONING THE LIGHT

My first experience of my own power against evil happened at the age of fifteen. I was living in Bristol, a city in England, and attending an all-girls school. I was a naive teenager with no life skills and little knowledge about the supernatural or how it could affect anyone. One afternoon my stepfather, who was in the army, strolled in from work and casually informed my mother and I that we would be departing England and setting sail for Malaysia, where we would live for the next three years. I was stunned; the bottom had just fallen out of my world. I would be leaving my grandparents, school, and friends, and living in a strange place on the other side of the world.

After three weeks at sea, we arrived in Ipoh, in the state of Perak, and settled into a spacious rented house. Mother excitedly began inspecting the rooms, starting with the kitchen. Curiously, she opened the cutlery drawer and stood frozen to the spot as a dozen giant cockroaches spewed out, dropped on the floor, and ran all over her feet. She shuddered in disbelief and then spent all day saying it was a bad omen.

Gradually, we settled into the new home, still trying to get used to our complete change of environment.

One night at 3 A.M., the heat was overpowering; the small bedside fan did little to help ease the situation. I was restless and on edge and finally drifted into an uneasy sleep. Suddenly, I sat bolt upright in the bed. For the first time in my life, I felt a spiritual presence warning me to be strong. Some years before, my grandmother had told me about spirit guides and how they could appear when situations go wrong. This thought immediately sprung to mind.

In the open doorway were five men, their eyes traveling all over me. Instinctively I knew there was a strong chance I would be raped. My stepfather was away on maneuvers in Borneo, and my mother and little brother slept peacefully in the next room. I could feel my heartbeat racing in blind panic, but the voice inside my head said, "Fight back, Beleta, use your defense skills." My mind was screaming, "What defense skills... what the hell are defense skills?" Suddenly, it was as if something was taking over my body, and balancing on my knees, I was filled with invisible strength; this mighty power began surging through me. I stared at the men with such disdain, then in a firm but controlled voice, I spat, "Get *out, get out, get out now!" Psychic energy was permeating all around me, and then suddenly, a pale lavender light entered my crown chakra and proceeded to move down through my body; it made a crackling noise that created some electrical force. I'm unsure if the intruders saw the light, but they all looked terrified. They turned on their heels and immediately fled.*

When they left, I started to cry, and then a stillness came over the room and a soft voice in my head said, "Well done."

Later, when the police came to investigate, they said how lucky we were, as this gang of men had killed an English woman only two weeks earlier when they raided her home.

If you have spiritual faith and are faced with a dangerous situation like the one described above, you can instantaneously call for spiritual protection by using mind power.

However frightened you might feel, try to keep as calm as possible and in your mind, ask your spirit helpers to assist you, or if you are in a hazardous situation, summon Archangel Michael, the most powerful protector of all. For more information about guides and angels, please see page 196.

Part II

HAUNTINGS

GHOSTS OR SPIRIT ENTITIES THAT haven't passed over may sometimes attach themselves to the living and invade their space. In this chapter, we will explore the most common hauntings that may occur and offer different resolutions.

The majority of the time, ghostly activity is associated with homes or other buildings, but in reality, any natural location or space can have a spirit presence linked to it. It's also not uncommon for ghosts and apparitions to haunt specific people, and no matter how many times they move, they will follow them from house to house.

There are many different types of ghosts; some are just imprinting on time, nothing more than a residual energy force that plays out like a recording of a past event, and others are trying to interact with those still living. When a person dies inexplicably, their spirit may continue to exist and haunt the building or area where they formerly resided.

Every faith has its version of post-death beliefs, and although some differ considerably, there is usually an underlying theme. In truth, very few people know what happens to our souls when we die. Religious people tend to have deep-seated beliefs based on their faith. Others will trust their instincts, do research, and ultimately come to their own conclusions. Those who have had near-death experiences or individuals who have undergone hypnosis have shed light on a spirit world of beauty. They tell of traveling through a portal to another dimension and meeting with loved ones and cherished pets. The body we occupy in life is merely a vessel to carry us around while we live on planet Earth. A good analogy is to liken yourself to an automobile; you step into the car at birth, drive around in it for as many years as you are allocated, and once the vehicle breaks down, you step out of it.

Medical professionals such as physicians and nurses who deal with death on a daily basis have even described witnessing a soul leaving its physical body. A translucent apparition or a yellow light may occasionally be seen floating upward from a person's body or hanging over the person's head.

CASE STUDY: LEANNA HYPNOSIS

My stepfather is a trained clinical hypnotherapist, and many years ago, I was so curious about reincarnation, I went through a spell of being regressed so that I might visit my past lives. Although I consider myself a spiritual person, I'm a Taurean, very down-to-earth, and have my feet planted firmly on the ground. For me, rather than having blind faith, I needed proof, so, throughout these regressions, I would check out my findings on ancestry websites to see whether my hypnotic experiences were, in fact, accurate and not just put down to an overactive imagination. Unfortunately, many of my past life experiences were disjointed and unclear throughout these sessions, and I could only recall snippets of information. As you can imagine, this was quite frustrating, especially as hypnotherapy can sometimes take hours. However, one such regression was very interesting. I asked my stepfather to take me deep into the hypnosis, and I saw myself in Londonderry, Ireland, during the potato famine. The timeline was around the mid-1800s, and I was living with my then father and two brothers. My name was Katherine Hawkings, and we were struggling to feed ourselves. To cut a long story short, I married a man who looked very much like my husband today. We decided to emigrate to Canada, where I lived out the remainder of my life on a ranch. After the regression, I searched for

*my former self on an ancestry website. I actually found Kath-
erine who resided in Londonderry, and followed her story—I
even saw her ship's passage to Canada. For me, this was all
the proof I needed.*

*After this experience, I was driven to learn more about
the purpose of life and to discover what happens to a person's soul when they die. I asked my stepfather if we could
experiment. Instead of visiting previous incarnations under
hypnosis, I suggested that we travel back to a precise time
just before my birth so that I could discover the answers to
my questions.*

*Before the hypnosis, my stepfather programmed my sub-
conscious to remember everything I learned during the ses-
sion. It took around an hour to get me into a deep enough
hypnotic state, but soon after, I saw a vision of a man in white
who told me he was my guide, Peter, and that he had been
with me through this life and most of my previous incarnations
on Earth. It was a strange sensation because his face was so
familiar, and I knew I hadn't seen him for a very long time. It
was like meeting a friend from the past that you had forgot-
ten all about. Of course, I knew this was my opportunity to ask
questions, so I asked him all I wanted to know. I was expecting him to answer me directly, but he didn't. I can only explain
that it was akin to telepathic communication. While I con-
versed with Peter, he told me that before every life, a soul is
programmed not to remember the time it spends in the spirit
world. Of course, I asked why, and he replied that if we knew
the purpose of life before visiting Earth, we couldn't learn firsthand the lessons we'd be given. It dawned on me then that
everything a person experiences is all about spiritual growth.
We must keep repeating the reincarnation process to resonate
on a higher vibration. The whole thing made sense to me.*

*While I was there, I also questioned Peter about religion.
He went on to tell me that there is no such thing as religion in
the spirit realms but that it was of great importance on Earth.
To have faith, whatever it may be, helps the soul to focus and*

ascend. It is unimportant what belief system a person chooses to follow, but it brings like-minded souls together, those on the same vibrational frequency. I asked the question: If religion doesn't exist in the spirit realms, wouldn't the souls of the departed be disappointed upon death to find they had dedicated their life to something that doesn't exist? He answered simply, and said that if someone, for example, were a devout Christian, their afterlife would be shaped into everything they wanted, so if they were expecting Jesus to welcome them after death, that is precisely what would happen to them.

If a person is kind, sensitive, and has led a decent, straightforward life, upon death, the spirit of the individual usually has no trouble ascending to the spirit world. After a period of adjustment, we must reflect on the life we have just lived, and although our spiritual helpers do not judge us for any misgivings, we do, in truth, judge ourselves. He told me this could be a very emotional experience for the soul because, before our incarnation, we might have been full of good intentions and planned on embracing our future life in a certain way. Of course, good intentions are great in theory, especially in a beautiful nirvana environment full of motivation and surrounded by our spirit guides encouraging us. It's a very different scenario when we reincarnate, as earthly life is complex and tedious at times, and we are often faced with dealing with more than one difficult situation at a time.

When we reincarnate, we may fail specific preordained lessons, and then once we die and begin scrutinizing the life we have just lived, we can feel as though we have let ourselves down. Every experience encountered in life, as with every person we associate with, is preplanned before we are born. We are given an itinerary of lessons we must complete to help our souls evolve. If you fail some of these lessons or sidestep the path you are destined to follow, the sense of failure is very apparent.

Peter told me that there is another reason why we try so hard to pass our life lessons. We all belong to an individual soul group, a selection of souls we repeatedly reincarnate with; this made sense, and I realized that in my Irish life, my husband now was, in fact, my husband then. There can often be up to twenty souls in one group, each having to experience similar lessons. If a few of the souls in the group elevate their vibration quickly, the other souls can be left behind; this is a real fear amongst the souls of the departed, so if you are unsuccessful in your life's quests, you will have to come back, reincarnating again and again until you learn the lesson in completion. Sometimes, you may have to reincarnate hundreds of times to correct one flaw in your character. There is no time limit to complete these quests, but it does depend on each individual whether they choose to embrace their lessons or not.

You might wonder what this has to do with hauntings or psychic attacks, but it does help us to realize why some souls fail to pass over at the end of their life and continue to be anchored to Earth. Many who have not made the best out of their life or those who hinder or harm others could fear crossing over because they don't want to face their judgment. According to Peter, there are many different spirit realms on the other side, and they reflect the kind of soul you are. There is no heaven or hell per se; the soul's final destination reflects the nature of the departed's spirit. If you were a decent human being who tried their best to help others in life, your spirit home might be beautiful, with rolling fields and stunning scenery. Those who are selfish, abusive, corrupt, and harm others might end up in a place that reflects their nature, which would be a much darker place with little comfort. These individuals can only venture into the higher realms once their souls have matured enough. Their only way out is to keep reincarnating and to experience some of the situations they may have inflicted on others in their previous incarnation; the theory is your soul cannot truly understand something until you have experienced it firsthand.

Each soul will have to know what it's like to be wealthy, live in poverty, work extremely hard, or have a life of leisure. All, at some point or another, will suffer from disability so that they can empathize entirely with those who struggle with these kinds of problems.

Often, we agree before we are born to live amongst those from different soul groups; this could explain why some people feel they are nothing like their family members on Earth or stick out as the black sheep of the family. A more mature soul might agree to reincarnate with someone from a lower vibrational group to help them ascend quicker.

CROSSING OVER

MILLIONS OF SOULS FAIL TO cross over upon death; each will have their own spirit guide who will patiently assist them in making that journey. Because we are born with free will, it's up to us whether we want to head toward the light. If a deceased spirit is hesitant or, for whatever reason, fears their afterlife, they will root themselves to the Earth plane and refuse to cross over. Some souls, upon death, can be confused and won't accept or even realize that they are dead, whereas others won't move on because they have unfinished business on Earth. Those sensitive, mediumistic people who can tap into ethereal energies can sense, see, and even converse with them.

Karma is also essential to the soul's evolution. For example, suppose a person doesn't care that someone is struggling with a mental health issue, or they might step over an unhoused person in the street who is crying out for help. In that case, they must reincarnate into that situation to fully understand the lesson. Before reaching the ultimate level of spiritual evolvement, we must undergo and understand every human emotion possible.

At the end of the day, it's how you handle your life and treat others that really matters.

I learned so much from Peter when I was under hypnosis that it warrants a book of its own, but for now, with my feet firmly on the ground, I'm a believer!

PARANORMAL PORTALS

A GHOSTLY PORTAL IS LIKE a swirling energy disc separating one dimension from another. Many negative spirit entities are believed to reside in an alternative realm adjacent to our Earth plane. These beings are said to be able to enter our world only if a portal between the two realms opens. There are millions of open portals around the Earth where unwanted spirits can wander, and new ones are constantly popping up. These areas are energetic hot spots, mainly situated on ley lines, which are electromagnetic angles around the Earth, appearing where any concentrated energy has formed. According to one hypothesis, there are two types of portals: entrances and exits. Exit portals can exist where death has occurred en masse, such as hospitals, battlegrounds, or around locations where many people have died simultaneously. Once a spirit has traveled through one of these portals, it cannot return via the same route, as it can only pass through them in one direction. Any number of things can create entrance portals. Geological events, such as weather patterns and earthquakes, even solar flares, can generate enough energy to open one. A more common way is if people who are unfamiliar or untrained with occult practices decide to conduct a séance out of curiosity or a bit of fun. By doing this, they unknowingly create an entrance portal that is often difficult to close. Evil or demonic entities can become trapped here on the Earth plane, creating havoc for everyday people.

EXTRADIMENSIONAL DEMONS

SOME BELIEVE THAT DEMONS ARE extradimensional creatures who feed off a human's fear, which makes the entity stronger and more powerful. They are far more malevolent than ordinary spirits, and possess so much strength they can physically touch or injure the living, causing scratches and bruises, and often drag their victims out of bed. Even small children are not spared as demons see them as easy targets. Powerful mediums or priests can send these formidable creatures back through exit portals, but it takes a great deal of skill and effort to succeed.

CASE STUDY: VIRGINIAROSE CENTRILLO
THE CLAPTON ANGELS

Virginiarose works for the Pennsylvania Paranormal Association with paranormal investigator Mark Keyes and has appeared on the TV shows *Paranormal Survivor* and *The Haunted*.

I was born a medium, have always been able to see ghosts and spirits, so I have spent over forty years helping those stuck on the Earth plane cross over into the light. When I was around twenty-five, I was helping a family in Connecticut who were experiencing ghostly activity in their home. I was young and inexperienced, and after connecting to the spirit, I realized it wasn't a ghost as such but some form of demonic entity that had attached itself to and possessed the woman's alcoholic husband. The husband had recently died, so the entity had nowhere to go. He couldn't cling to or possess anyone else in the house because they were God-fearing people, so he was roaming around, causing no end of havoc. I admit, this powerful demon was frightening, and although I didn't usually have a problem crossing over spirits, this was different, and I immediately knew I was out of my depth! I was struggling. I decided to sit in the room, do a deep meditation, and try to summon a higher power to help me remove this thing from their home. Suddenly, I had an out-of-body experience and was looking at myself, sitting on the chair. As soon as I did this, I could see the entity more clearly. At first, it appeared as a mass of gray and black smoke before it transitioned into a dark shadowy creature with cruel eyes and a sinister stare. It was vile!

Out of nowhere, I started to hear a tinny, metal-like sound. It sounded very similar to metal grating together or the sound cymbals leave behind after they've been crashed. An angel entered the room, dressed in bronze-looking armor with a helmet and face covering. Her eyes were the most beautiful emerald green shade I have ever seen; she looked almost robotic, but I knew she was some kind of celestial being be-cause I could see the feathers under the armor. In a mechanical voice, she said, "We are the Claptons," then, out of nowhere, another three appeared and formed a circle around me. Of course, I was speechless, but I knew I could trust them. Feel-ing helpless only a few moments before, I suddenly felt highly protected. One angel guided me out of the circle by the arm while another took out something similar to a golden lasso. She hurled it forward, capturing the demon, and pulled the entity forcefully through a wall and out of the window. After that, they were gone, and the home was free of its haunting.

Over the years, while cleansing houses, I frequently detect the slight sound of metal grinding, which tells me the Clap-ton angels are nearby. On occasions, I have even caught a glimpse of a metal wing in my peripheral vision.

My work with Mark and the team primarily includes go-ing to haunted places to rid them of ghosts and any other bad energy, and on many occasions, I see Saint Germain first, followed by the most majestic black panthers with the same beautiful emerald green eyes and then, finally, the Claptons. I do wonder if they are all connected. The panthers are pres-ent whenever I need to cross the spirits of children over; they nuzzle them before carrying them on their backs and into the light. They also help if a soul is having a tough time or if the person died by suicide, was murdered, or died from alcohol or a drug overdose.

After spending years attempting to identify these entities, I have a strong awareness that they may be extraterrestrial and possibly here to expel dark spirits that may have origi-nated from another planet. They are definitely not your typi-cal angels or guides.

SPIRIT BOARD OR OUIJA BOARD

THE KENNARD NOVELTY COMPANY IN America created this product for the first time in the 1890s, and as a result, they began to make a lot of money. Kennard said that the Ouija board was created as a parlor game and that the term "Ouija" meant "good luck." For numerous years, it outsold all other games, selling up to two thousand boards per week. Later, the film industry jumped on the bandwagon, and the horror movie *The Exorcist* was born, pushing up the sales of the Ouija board even further. The Ouija has a distinctive appearance, consisting of a board that shows all the letters of the alphabet; also included are the words "yes" and "no." A planchette, which is a small heart-shaped piece of wood with wheeled casters on the underside, is situated on the top of the board. Individuals place their fingers on the planchette until it moves around the board independently, spelling out the answers to any questions that have been asked. Generally, the aim of the game is for individuals to connect with deceased family members; perhaps they want to contact a mother, husband, or sibling. Although it is, in fact, possible to summon dead relatives through the board, the lower vibrational entities, who are basically a stone's throw away on an adjacent plane, know how to entice a person into their space by tricking them into believing they are speaking directly to a deceased loved one. They are literally lying in wait for an invitation to cross over. These spirits are typically demonic, although ghosts of those who have failed to cross over into the spirit world can also come through and haunt the home.

In other circumstances, a demonic spirit will attach itself to a person rather than a building and follow them around for years, even after they have moved locations. Dark shadows might appear in the home, foul smells will come out of nowhere, and some of the most experienced paranormal investigators and mediums will fail to send the creature back from whence it came.

When someone invites spirits into their home, there is usually a price to be paid, especially for those who are experimenting and have no real idea of the consequences. What seems like a bit of fun at first might have serious repercussions. The entities can go on to create havoc in the home, throwing things, smashing crockery, banging doors, and scaring the occupants half to death. Some are so evil they can levitate humans, rape, or even possess them. As we have mentioned above, the entities draw strength from human fear, so they can become untouchable after a while.

INVITING IN DEMONS

A MORE DETERMINED AND EMPOWERED spirit will attempt what is known as a walk-in, a process where the spirit will try to take control of an individual's body and leave them possessed. The entity will invade a person's body to such an extent that it will even speak through its human vessel. Some may argue that the possessed suffers from a mental health condition and put it down to some form of hysteria, but this doesn't explain much of the physical evidence. Victims can vomit black mucus and take on a different appearance altogether. In situations like this,

Catholic priests are often brought in to exorcise the individual using powerful prayer and holy water; this has been successful over the centuries, as demons hate anything to do with religion and God.

These stories are not just made up for effect. They are very real and happen constantly throughout the world. Although our grandmother did experiment with the spirit board and participated in numerous séances, we prefer to caution people today about the associated risks. Our recommendation is to steer clear!

PSYCHIC WORK

ENTRANCE PORTALS CAN ALSO APPEAR as a result of any psychic practice; this can be Tarot readings, medium readings, palmistry, psychometry, automatic writing, and, believe it or not, even meditation. Most of the information given to a psychic reader will come directly from the spirit world, and to gain access to this information, one has to open a doorway and invite them in. Mediums' homes can often be active, and spirits communicating with their loved ones through a medium can sometimes linger around for a few days.

SOLUTION

BEFORE YOU BEGIN PSYCHIC WORK, you need to ensure you create the right energy in the room, so lighting some white candles and playing meditative music is an excellent idea. A small silent prayer in advance will also focus your mind on receiving positive messages from guides and loved ones in spirit. Something like:

> *"I ask that only positive spirits communicate with me today. I do not recognize evil; I will not tolerate evil. Only the purest of spirits are welcome. Spirits, I ask that you protect me in my work and shield me with light."*

After psychic work, it is essential to open the window in the room you have been working in and let the fresh air blow through for at least ten minutes. Any residual energy should dissipate. Keep a white tealight candle burning for a while and light some dragon's blood incense while saying this incantation:

> *"I ask the higher realms to cleanse this space from all things supernatural. Bathe this room in light and love. My work here today is complete."*

BLACK MAGIC

NOT EVERYONE WHO PRACTICES WITCHCRAFT has the best intentions, and those practitioners who prefer to cast their magic on the edge of good are famous for opening doorways into the darker realms. Selfish magic with no regard for others or spells cast with an adverse frame of mind can create enough negative energy to generate a portal. Witches who practice white magic only tend to connect with positive universal energies, and this is unlikely to tap into any hostile forces. More often than not, those who might dabble in witchcraft for a bit of fun may later live to regret it, especially if they accidentally conjure some dark spirit who decides to attach themselves to them. Our advice here is to only participate in spellcasting if you are well-informed. For more information on spell craft and magic, Leanna has written many books on the subject.

SOLUTION

TO COUNTERACT THE EFFECTS OF black magic, we might have to partake in white magic to fix the problem. Most of the time, dark practitioners will use the power of the mind to influence a situation, so you must keep your thoughts and mindset pure and free of negativity. If you need to perform a spell, remember that evil finds it difficult to connect to anything truly positive. Some of the solutions in this book will involve a ritual of some kind. Follow them as directed, and you should be able to offset any black magic attack.

SPIRIT BOXES

TODAY, GHOST DETECTION SOFTWARE, INCLUDING spirit boxes, is still a novel idea. However, spirit boxes are effective, and when utilized properly in haunted places, they can facilitate contact between the living and the dead. In some instances, paranormal researchers and mediums have even assisted a ghost in transitioning back to the spirit world. However, if a person uses it in their home for a bit of fun, they might end up opening an unwanted portal.

MIRRORS

MIRRORS AND PORTALS HAVE LONG been the subjects of superstition, with some believing they serve as doorways for ghosts and demons. Some consider it unsafe to place two mirrors facing each other; this could be challenging, especially if you run a barbershop or hair salon. However, these kinds of locations are frequently haunted. It is always best to limit mirrors to one in a room at any time, or if you want more, place them all facing the same direction; this doesn't apply to using the small, tiled mirrors that face outward in your windows to reflect the evil eye.

There is a very easy way to establish whether your mirror is acting as a portal. Press your finger to the glass, and should you see a space between your finger and its reflection, your mirror is, in fact, a spiritual gateway. If this is the case, remove it from the house immediately to prevent further spirits from entering your home or building.

CLOSING A PORTAL

WHEN YOU WANT TO CLOSE a portal, you must first establish whether it's an entrance or an exit. Exits don't need to be closed as they pose no threat to the living; these are purely gateways to the spirit world, where a dead person goes through shortly after death. Entrances, however, do need to be closed and secured. First, you must determine where the opening is. Is the haunting only in one room, or is it widespread throughout the property? If this is the case, there might be more than one portal. Some spirits will remain only in the room with a gateway, and others will wander, haunting every room in the house, so a thorough investigation beforehand is necessary. You will need a pendulum or any weighted object on a chain to find the gateway. The type of metal or crystal is unimportant. Start in the room where you are experiencing most of the activity and close all windows and doors; this will ensure no drafts are moving the pendulum to give you a false reading.

Stand with the pendulum in front of you with the chain in your fingers at arm's length. Walk slowly around the room, pausing every couple of steps. Keep your arm as still as possible when you stop so your body movement doesn't interrupt the swing.

If the chain begins to move on its own, take note of the direction in which it circles. If it is rotating clockwise, this indicates an entrance portal. Anticlockwise represents an exit. It's not unusual for portals to be high up in the air or adjacent to walls. You might also notice a drop in temperature in certain parts of the room; this is a sure sign you are in the vicinity of the portal, and you can now begin to close it.

The most effective way is through prayer or the summoning of spirit helpers. To do this, you might hold a lit white candle in a suitable holder and say something like:

> *"I ask the positive spirits to close this doorway, allowing no negative forces to pass through. Cast out any evil spirits, leaving this space free of negativity. Protect this home and all who dwell here."*

Another safe method is burning sage, which has exceptional cleansing properties and is believed to clear houses of hauntings. Some people with a good knowledge of this subject consider that dragon's blood, a resin from the *Croton lechleri* tree in the Amazon rainforest, outperforms sage. Like the sage bundle (smudging stick), it will disinfect and close the doorway when burned. Using the two together, simultaneously burning the sage and dragon's blood, is highly effective.

Religious folks use holy water to seal gateways and sanitize an area. You can accomplish this by spraying water on the region where you believe the gateway to be. Even better, spray it around the house.

Another excellent technique is visualization. Close your eyes and visualize the gateway closing as you stand in front of the portal's location. You can draw the walls of the doorway together with your hands and your mind by moving your arms in an outward to inward motion. Keep doing this until you feel satisfied that it is securely closed. When a portal is shut, the atmosphere in the room will lift, and you'll get a strong sense of peace. The room may also appear visibly brighter like the sun is shining through the windows. If you still feel uneasy, then continue with the actions above.

Remember, to have the best success in closing these gateways is to have the right intent. Be very specific and believe wholeheartedly that you will close this entrance, even demand it to be forever sealed, and it should work.

Even after successfully closing a portal, any demon or hostile ghost that arrives through it cannot return the same way, so your house could still remain haunted, and you will need to take extra measures to banish it.

BLUE BUBBLE PROTECTION

WHEN AN INDIVIDUAL FEELS REALLY threatened by a demonic entity, there is a temporary fix that can be used wherever they are. Try to go somewhere private; the bathroom is always a good place. Gel the hands with sanitizer or wash them thoroughly. Closing your eyes, take ten deep breaths, exhaling slowly. Now imagine a vivid blue bubble slowly traveling up from the feet and encompassing your whole body. This will act as your protective coat for the whole day.

TYPES OF HAUNTINGS

MANY PEOPLE WORLDWIDE CLAIM TO have felt the presence of a ghost, spirit, or even a deceased loved one. Some may dismiss it as an overactive imagination or wishful thinking, but in many situations, particularly among those who believe in a hereafter, for them, it's a very real experience. We were all born with a sixth sense, and whether we choose to listen to these instincts varies from person to person. Some embrace these emotions, and others have the door firmly closed to them. A person can detect any anomalous energy that might be lingering in a place, and those who are sensitive to this are more likely to see or feel the presence of a ghost than those who are not.

It's crucial to keep in mind that you don't need to see a ghost to believe in its existence. We've both experienced unusual feelings when visiting haunted places throughout the years, and have even lived in haunted houses.

HOW TO TELL IF YOUR
HOUSE IS HAUNTED

PARANORMAL INVESTIGATOR MARK KEYES, AUTHOR of *The Upper Darby Poltergeist* and *Chasing Shadows: A Criminal Investigator's Look into the Paranormal*, kindly shared with us some of his experiences recording ghostly activities with his team. Mark, who has a degree in psychology, worked as a criminal investigator for twenty-five years and always considered himself an optimistic skeptic regarding anything paranormal. After retiring from the force, he began researching ghosts and hauntings and founded the Pennsylvania Paranormal Association. He has since taken part in TV shows such as *Paranormal 911*, *Haunted Hospitals*, and *Paranormal Survivor*.

Although he travels to numerous locations in an effort to help people rid their homes of spirits, he informed us that demonic beings are not that common and more often than not, the occupants are witnessing ghostly activity.

COLD SPOTS

WHETHER IT be spirits or demons, it is common to feel chilly spots around the house. Because these concentrated areas exist around the ghost, you may experience a shiver if you walk through a vicinity where a spirit is standing, or you may feel a cold, clammy sensation if they walk toward you. Some people have even claimed to have seen their own chilly breath. According to Mark, the temperature can drop by up to ten degrees in a matter of seconds when a ghost is nearby.

IS SOMEONE THERE?

SENSITIVE OR psychic people might occasionally feel like someone is watching them, especially if they're alone in the house. Feeling as if you are being scrutinized is standard, as ghosts and spirits are naturally fascinated with the living and will try to communicate with us by making their presence known somehow. If you're in tune with your sixth sense, you will instantly feel on the alert, as if someone is observing you; this could occur early in the morning when you wake up to use the bathroom, or you could feel uneasy walking up the stairs and get the feeling something or someone is waiting for you at the top. At best, these sensations are creepy; this is typical ghostly behavior, especially if you have recently relocated to a new property that happens to have a few spirits in situ. The ghosts will be naturally curious about the new residents.

SMELLS AND SCENTS

IF A DECEASED LOVED ONE is close, they can manifest themselves by emitting fragrances similar to a favorite perfume. If they smoked, you might notice a smell of tobacco, or in some cases, a meal cooking. It isn't uncommon to experience a sickly sweet stench or a foul odor if the spirit is demonic or disruptive.

When a loved one or family member dies, the deceased's home or dwelling may have a different energy. As previously said, there may be chilly patches or strong smells, or you may feel like someone else is in the house with you. According to some theorists, once a soul departs from its earthly body, the deceased's ghost may remain around their family or friends for up to three weeks following their death. It is believed in many faiths that they are escorted by a spirit guide who will eventually assist them in making the gentle transition into the spirit realm. Even if they do pass over immediately, it is not uncommon for them to return to the Earth plane and attend their own funeral.

HAUNTING DREAMS

WHEN A LOVED ONE PASSES away, it is common for the deceased to visit the dreams of those they have left behind shortly after death. Because our subconscious vibration is higher when we are in a dreamlike state, spirits find it much simpler to communicate with us. They will often appear to comfort their family or let them know their soul lives on. Still, these dreams may occasionally be disturbing, especially if the spirit is unsettled by their passing or has to communicate with you before they can rest in peace. These reveries can occur every night until they feel ready to move on.

If your house is haunted, unfavorable ghosts can also haunt your dreams. As a result, you might experience terrifying nightmares with blood, gore, and other unmentionable things. Demons invade dreams because when we sleep, we are vulnerable and easy to manipulate; they are bullies that like to pick on the weakest.

One of the most unsettling indicators of a haunting is when a person is about to fall asleep and hears someone calling out their name. There may be occasions when you hear other words being uttered, like part of a sentence or someone laughing. When a person drifts into sleep, the mind and soul enter a state of altered consciousness, which might expose you to any spirit, good or evil.

Often, an ugly face or demonic image appears behind their closed eyes. People frequently claim that their imagination could never conjure up such a picture, which is often true. Lower-level entities can home in and expose themselves when one is in this semi-sleep state. This doesn't necessarily mean that the house is haunted, but more likely the sleepy person is giving off an energetic light, and the demon is drawn to it like a moth to a flame; this happens a lot with people who are psychic or mediumistic.

IS SOMEONE IN MY BED?

A PERSON WILL SENSE SOMEONE sitting on their bed or cuddling up behind them as they fall asleep; this might be a loved one in spirit, the soul of a departed pet, a ghost haunting the property, or an evil entity wanting to terrify them. You will instinctively know if it's malevolent because you'll be fearful. Deceased loved ones send a more positive vibe to the recipient that does not frighten them. Over the years, there have been several tales of obstructive spirits ripping off the bedsheets. Some of them have even been caught on video cameras.

NOISES AND BANGS

WHEN A GHOST OCCUPIES THE same space as you, you may hear strange noises that appear to originate from nowhere; tapping, loud bangs, or even speaking might be heard. Some people may hear these conversations in the distance or footsteps moving up and down the stairs. The ghosts of children can be very noisy and can often be heard running around on a higher floor of the house. Occasionally they might laugh or cry. Demons might growl like dogs or have a lower tone to their voice, and it's not unusual for them to shout and curse or repeatedly tell you to get out!

ELECTRONIC INTERFERENCE

GHOSTS AND SPIRITS OFTEN AFFECT the electricity or batteries in a house. Lights may flicker on and off or dip for a few seconds. A crackling or pinging sound can accompany this. In some cases, appliances can turn themselves on and off. For instance, the TV, computer, or radio might suddenly spring into action, or the kettle may boil on its own. Some spirits have even been known to turn on a torch or flashlight in response to any questions that might be asked of them.

PROTECTION

TO AVOID BEING A VICTIM, putting protection in place before going to sleep is the only way to keep out anything sinister. Visualization is particularly helpful. When you close your eyes, silently pray and ask your guide or deity to protect you while you are sleeping. Next, imagine your body being bathed in an impenetrable bright white light pulsating with each heartbeat. Keep this vision in your mind for as long as you can.

Using profanity might not be for everyone, but weirdly, it really works, and the creature will immediately disappear; if you are experiencing the images of demons or ugly monsters, you need to be confident and tell it with force to fuck off. This probably works because, as we have already mentioned, demons tend to focus on the weak, frightened, or vulnerable. By demonstrating mental strength this way, the entity won't bother to waste its energy on someone who shows no fear. We have both encountered this kind of psychic attack in the past and can confirm this method of dealing with them works every time.

THE LEMON TEST

LEMONS ABSORB NEGATIVE ENERGY, SO if you think your house is haunted by a spirit or demon, place a whole lemon in every room of your home. After a week, look at the skin of the lemon, and if it has dark, pitted marks or is changing color in any way, it's a sure sign that you have a spirit entity in your house. If the skin remains yellow and shows no sign of decay, your home is clean.

ASTRAL PROJECTION AND WALK-INS

HAVE YOU EVER FALLEN ASLEEP and woken up feeling like you were about to fall? Astral projection occurs when the soul leaves the body and wanders in and around other planes of existence or visits alternative dimensions. We've talked about how our soul enters a different level of consciousness when we sleep, but many people can go to the next stage with or without knowing it.

During a projection, rather than the soul floating up and out of the body, it drops in a swift, downward motion and then gently rises on one side of the body; this initial drop gives the person the sensation of falling. When one masters the art of astral projection, it can be an exhilarating feeling. Dreams of flying very fast or running at speed leave a person elated and keen to try it again.

During this experience, it is believed that the soul is still attached to the body by an invisible silver cord that is indestructible until death takes place. Imagine a spaceman floating in outer space while connected to his umbilical cable. Without it, he would drift into the ether. Our silver cord serves the same purpose, but even with the cord in place, a person is still exposed because this is the ideal time for a malicious spirit to set up residence in their body. The entity can occupy a body for years, living alongside a person's soul, without ever being discovered. Gradually it can manipulate and control their mind and actions and disrupt their mental health. Their personality could be changeable, perhaps becoming aggressive or abusive or showing signs of a dual personality.

When a person is deeply asleep, the soul sometimes leaves the body and seeks freedom for new experiences. There are many places to visit, all with different themes and vibrations. Some are stunningly beautiful and spiritual, whereas others can be sinister, with lower entities and demons waiting to pounce.

As a sidebar, the soul can also visit the Akashic records to view the life lessons in place at that time, which could be helpful in their present life. The Akashic records can remind one of the mysteries of a person's faults, strengths, and current karmic lessons to improve the soul, especially in fighting back negativity from other entities or those who wish to harm them.

Before settling down for sleep, protective methods must be established so that unseen forces cannot take over your body. Walk-ins typically occur between 3 A.M. and 4 A.M., which some people consider the witching hour. Combining the crystals fluorite, tiger's eye, and black obsidian will create a powerful energy field around the sleeper, so wear a bracelet made of these crystals or keep the three stones under your pillow.

CASE STUDY: BELETA
NIGHT WATCH

Leanna has this gift, but knowing how vulnerable any kind of astral projection can leave a person, she doesn't perform it often. Once when I was ill, she transported herself to me in the early hours and sat on my bed for around twenty minutes to see if I was okay. I had no experience of her visit, but she told me the exact time my husband came in to check on me, and after speaking to him, he confirmed she was right. Another time she traveled to Scotland, where my husband and I were on vacation. When we got home, she relayed her visit to me and described the new floral pajamas I was wearing. There was no way she would have known about them because I had purchased them that morning from a Scottish store. She also commented on my irritability and that I couldn't sleep properly in the heat as there was no fan, which was true. I didn't know whether to be cross with her for the intrusion or stunned that she could just come and see me at will. She laughed and said she would always make sure I had bathroom privacy!

BOOZE AND SUBSTANCES

DRUGS AND ALCOHOL CAN CAUSE havoc to the dreamer as they can alter the true consciousness of the person, leaving them wide open to walk-ins and psychic attacks. When a person is significantly impaired by drugs or alcohol, their soul may drift in and out of their body, similar to astral projection. Discarnate spirits always lurk around to take over a body that's not in control, so possession can occur. Like with other possessions, the creature can continue to live inside the person, sometimes for the rest of their life. Often, the victim goes mad as the entity gradually takes over their thoughts, feelings, and mental health.

REMOTE VIEWING

SCIENTIFICALLY THERE IS NO PROOF of remote viewing, so it is generally regarded as pseudoscience. In earlier occult studies, it was better known as telesthesia, ESP, and out-of-body travel. However, some believe that with the help of meditation and visualization, a medium or psychically talented individual can use remote viewing to astral travel to any location of their choosing. Remote viewers can use their skills to visualize events that have occurred in the past or the present day. Many secretly work alongside the police, solving crime, seeking out classified documents, and tapping into government secrets. One famous case was when a well-known medium performed a remote viewing of the dark side of the moon to reveal its secrets. Once they reported back, they were immediately hushed up.

Most psychics will make a detailed report of their findings as a form of proof for the skeptics.

CASE STUDY: BELETA
NIGHTTIME VISITORS

It is a recognized fact that most psychics don't always rest very well, often drifting in and out of sleep, but there is a trade-off as this can aid dream analysis and premonition.

Many years ago, a client came for a reading, and she had kindly purchased a book for me by a well-known guru. I looked at the picture of him on the front cover and shuddered. I questioned why I disliked a person who had millions worldwide following him. With the money lavished on him, I knew he had done much for humanity and animals, so why did I feel this way? Right from an early age, I had been given the gift of reading people's faces, which always put me in good stead. I had another restless night a few weeks later, but I suddenly fell into a trancelike state and saw this famous guru standing in a corner. He was wearing a long, white robe, his arms were folded across his chest, and he was staring at me intently. He had the gift of remote viewing, and I felt he was using his power on me. Immediately, he was aware that my defenses had sprung into action to block him, and he was surprised he'd been spotted. How had he heard of me, as I had no fame from TV or books then? I was angry that he had invaded my personal space, and I told him in no uncertain terms to bugger off! To my relief, he disappeared instantly.

A few years later, he was in the tabloids, and it was reported he had acted inappropriately with many young boys. He never got charged for his crime, as it wasn't proven, even though there was plenty of evidence; still, deep in my soul, I felt the accusations were true, which was why he made me recoil all those years ago. He's gone to his grave now, so the mystery remains, but I always trust my truth.

CASE STUDY: PATRICIA
THE HAUNTED PUB

Shortly after leaving college, I got a job as a cook in a busy pub in our town. The place was famous for being haunted and had a regular staff turnover because the workers would be too frightened to stay there. One evening after closing the kitchen for the night, I double-checked that all appliances were turned off before switching off the lights and closing the door. I sat at the bar, chatting with my boss, when I noticed a light shining from under the kitchen door. I quickly got up to investigate, and when I entered, every gas ring was on, the grill was smoking, and the microwave was lit up and rotating around and around. My boss wasn't surprised and said it happened all the time.

FROM THE CORNER OF YOUR EYE

FROM TIME TO TIME, YOU may see something in your peripheral vision, such as a shadow or a brief outline of a person. When you turn around quickly to look again, it will vanish. The only people who can see spirits are those who have some psychic ability; therefore, if this has happened to you, it may indicate that you have a mediumistic skill but haven't developed it enough to see the ghost for a sustained period of time.

MISSING OBJECTS

MISSING OBJECTS OR ITEMS CAN be attributed to simple forgetfulness, but a ghost often moves something in the home to attract attention. These missing items might be found in an unusual location, days or even weeks later; this is particularly common when the spirits of children are haunting a property. An example might be if a person puts their keys on a table and seconds later turns around to see they are gone. They can search the house from top to bottom, only to find them exactly where they left them.

CASE STUDY: LEANNA
THE SEWING BOX

We used to have a large stand-alone sewing box made of wood, and one day, we noticed one of the legs had fallen off. My father glued the leg on and left it to set. Later he went back to check the box and noticed that the leg had disappeared into the ether. We searched the house from top to bottom but couldn't find it anywhere. Frustratedly, he carried the sewing box back to the walk-in cabinet and carefully balanced it there so it wouldn't topple over. A few weeks later, Mother opened the box for some cotton and a needle, and the leg was placed neatly inside!

APPORTS

APPORTS ARE SMALL, INCONSPICUOUS OBJECTS like a sliver of crystal, a bead, or a charm that will materialize out of nowhere, usually in areas like the middle of a floor, the center of a table, or even the bed linen. They tend to emerge around mediumistic or psychic people, so many clairvoyants will discover them shortly after performing a reading for someone. However careful you are to put the apport somewhere safe, it can some-times vanish as quickly as it appeared. Although it's unclear if apports are "ghost or guide given," they can be typical in a psychic's home and commonplace in a haunted house.

CASE STUDY: BELETA
GIFTS FROM ABOVE

A few years ago, I was fast asleep at 3 A.M. when I heard beads clattering and cascading over the hardwood floor in my bedroom. Putting on the bedside lamp, I got up to in-spect what the noise was, and incredibly there was at least a handful of rose quartz, moonstone, amethyst, and pearl beads. Trembling, I scooped them up and put them on the bed, looking at them in amazement. A wise shamanic woman once told me about apports and how they can be given and taken, but I never believed in them until that night. The fol-lowing day, I threaded them to make a bracelet and got my husband to take a photo of it in case it disappeared. To this day, I still have this treasured gift, and I wear it often, espe-cially if I need spiritual protection.

INJURIES AND MARKS
ON THE BODY

ALTHOUGH LESS PREVALENT, EVIL SPIRITS and ghosts can harm and injure the living. If a negative spirit haunts the house, a person might wake up with scratches on their flesh or welts on the skin. Often, these marks will appear without the person realizing it. If the attack is demonic, they will often make three marks, such as three scratches, three bites, or sometimes three puncture wounds. This happens because the demon is mocking the religious trinity of the Father, the Son, and the Holy Ghost.

However, there are incidences where someone is aware of the attack and might be pushed or jostled. Afterward, an injury might appear on a particular part of their body; this often happens to paranormal investigators when they visit haunted locations.

PROTECTION

CHAKRA BALANCING

EVERY HUMAN has seven chakra points in their body starting with the crown, third eye, throat, heart, solar plexus, sacral, and root. These spinning discs of energy are connected to our body, emotions, and general well-being. When someone has been invaded or touched by a supernatural being, the energy points in the body can shift and become misaligned, so it's essential to realign these chakras to feel better again. Seeking a reputable crystal or Reiki healer to bring the chakras back into balance is the most effective way of restoring them. The healer might place certain crystals on the seven chakra points to ensure the energies flow correctly. This will really help the individual to start to heal.

SAGE SMUDGING

THIS BOOK frequently mentions sage since it is the go-to strategy for eliminating most supernatural activity. White sage smudging is a fantastic technique for removing undesirable energy from a person and from places, objects, or structures. It is also potent for driving away evil spirits and shutting down energetic hot spots. This ancient spiritual ritual originated with the Native Americans, but it has since been adopted and practiced by many other civilizations.

A smudging stick is simply a tightly bound bundle of dried sage fastened with string. It is lit and, when extinguished, emits lingering smoke. Sage is scientifically proven to sanitize the air and can kill the flu virus; however, it also works very well as a spiritual disinfectant to banish anything sinister. If you are sensitive to perfumes and incense, wear a mask because the smoke from the smudging stick can be overbearing.

If you believe you've been touched by a spirit or sense you have been cursed, you'll need someone to help you with this part. Stand up with your legs slightly apart and your arms stretched to the sides. Ask someone to waft the smoke over every part of your body; this can take a few minutes. If you're religious, you might like to say a prayer asking your deity to protect you; if not, you can call on spirit helpers by saying something like:

"I ask you to remove any negativity from my being. Protect me and encircle me in your light."

If several people have been affected by the spirit, smudge them all in the same way.

With hauntings or demonic activity, it's a good idea to smudge every room in the house and the family cars, garages, sheds, etc.

If this method fails, you must get the house blessed by a religious priest.

GHOSTS, DEMONS, AND LEGENDS

OUR HOME IS OUR SANCTUARY, so when things go bump in the night or we see something ghostly from the corner of our eye, it can leave us feeling petrified. So many different types of spirits can interact with the living, so it's not always easy to identify which kind you are up against. These phantom encounters range from regular ghosts that have failed to cross into the spirit world to demonic entities and disruptive poltergeists. It's not just ghosts and spirits that might haunt our space: Portals can open doorways to alternate dimensions, allowing other entities from adjacent worlds to make their presence known. These elemental beings or mythical figures that we sometimes read about in folklore can appear as fairies, sprites, goblins, ghouls, trolls, and vampires, to name a few. It is believed there are realms so close to the Earth plane that they overlap, so it's plausible that psychic people who can see otherworldly beings might encounter a mythical figure. Like demons, these supernatural creatures can be fascinated with the Earth plane and play their part in hauntings.

Every country and culture has its own versions of ghosts, spirits, and legendary myths, but in this section of the book, we will cover the common types people might expect to encounter.

RESIDUAL GHOSTS

RATHER THAN A GHOST, A residual haunting is a recurrence of a previous incident, comparable to a recording that may be played repeatedly, with the same events transpiring each time. The walls and foundations of a building can absorb events, both good and bad, that might then be played on the same day of the year or at the same time of day.

The witness might even hear noises or footsteps, perhaps screams or crying.

CASE STUDY: LAURA
HAUNTED COTTAGES

When I was a teenager in the 1980s, my parents relocated to Wiltshire and spent a year renting a very old cottage while they looked for a place to call their own. It was only after delving into some historical records that we realized the house was from the fifteenth century and was partly made of cob. Back in the day, it had served as a dairy to the larger house next door, and documents told how it had been used for smuggling in the 1600s. It was so tiny and atmospheric, but it didn't give off a bad vibe at all. The windowpanes in my room were original, and the room's walls were rounded. We knew it was haunted the moment we moved there because we would wake up to the aroma of freshly baked bread. Every day, we would hear footsteps walking around upstairs, and occasionally you could listen to conversations in the distance.

The cottage had a long, narrow country lane leading into a small cobbled courtyard, and one dusky evening, after saying goodbye to a friend, I walked back down the lane to return home. Suddenly from the right-hand side of me, I saw the transparent apparition of a large man wearing a wide-brimmed hat. I could only see the top half of his body as he strolled by, and he seemed not to notice me at all. I watched him walk into the courtyard and knew I had to go through that space to get home. I have never been more terrified in my life! Leanna and Beleta described this incident as a "residual" haunting, but I am sure the property housed more than one kind of ghost. Being a teenager, I often stayed out past my curfew, and one evening, I arrived home an hour late. My mother was furious. It was in the days before cell phones, and she was worried out of her mind. We started to row, voices were raised, and I was complaining and bemoaning about her unfairness when a voice bellowed throughout the cottage saying, "Bloody shut up!" It sounded like it was traveling down a tunnel, but it immediately silenced us.

INTELLIGENT HAUNTINGS

INTELLIGENT HAUNTINGS OCCUR WHEN A spirit interacts with the living. They can often appear as white apparitions or orbs and communicate visually or auditorily. For whatever reason, their soul has failed to pass over to the spirit realm, and they will try to attract the attention of the living to make themselves known. Interaction with the ghost can vary drastically depending on its power. You might only be able to hear one ghost but can visibly see another.

Sometimes, an intelligent ghost has unfinished business and won't pass over to the spirit realm until it's rectified. Often, because they are limited in their actions, the entity can be tied to a place and become disruptive or noisy. Virginiarose Centrillo, a psychic medium, says that communicating with these ghosts, learning what they desire, and trying to assist them in finding closure are some ways to get rid of them.

People have said in jest that they will haunt someone when they die, but this can often happen. Let's say the wife passes away and hangs around the living husband. He might go on to marry again, and the dead wife is distraught that her husband has moved on. Another example might be a deceased parent who refuses to cross over because the bond between them and their children is so strong. These spirits are "switched on" and focus solely on communicating with those around them.

People who have experienced this type of haunting describe hearing noises and bangs or footsteps. The ghost might want to raise attention by throwing inanimate objects across the room or making the lights flicker on and off.

An unfriendly or evil spirit might linger because they fear being judged after they die. If they were a harmful or wicked individual in life, they would continue to enjoy terrifying the living when disincarnate. These spirits will occupy a house or space, targeting those that might dwell there or come for a visit.

Many paranormal investigators use an EMF (electromagnetic field) meter or an EVP (electronic voice phenomenon) meter to connect with a ghost or entity. This sensitive equipment, alongside motion sensors, can detect the presence of otherworldly beings. In some cases, the investigators might ask the spirit a direct question, and when they play the EVP back later, there is an actual response to their question.

CASE STUDY: BELETA
THE CHINESE GRAVEYARD

After my marriage to Leanna's father, we lived in Malacca, Malaysia, and rented a spacious three-bedroom detached bungalow on the periphery of the army camp. I felt privileged as it had two bathrooms, three bedrooms, a servant's section, and an up-to-date kitchen with a large combined living and dining room. The rent was extremely cheap, and so we thought we'd fallen on our feet. Every day the grocery boy would arrive on his bicycle and take the daily food order. One day he casually remarked that no one ever stayed in the house for long, which was the reason for the low rent. Nervously I asked why, and he replied, "These bungalows are built on an ancient Chinese cemetery, and so they're haunted."

It didn't take long for the house to reveal its true colors. The first episode was at 3 P.M. one afternoon, and I went to the front door to call one of the dogs in. I shouted, "Coby, Coby," and then a disembodied, singsong voice whispered in my ear, "Coby, Coby!" As usual, I was alone as my husband was away in the jungle. That night I took the three dogs into my bedroom for protection and drifted into a troubled sleep. Suddenly, I awoke with a snap as all three animals approached an unseen entity in the corner of the room. Their hackles were up as they circled around, growling and snarling. To say it was a long night was an understatement, so we all went into the lounge for safety.

The next episode was just after dinner one evening, and the disincarnate voice was again in my ear. Laughing, it whispered, "Ants in the kitchen!" My husband was home this time, so we rushed into the kitchen to see hundreds of soldier ants swarming over the sink and drainers. The British army always provided insect sprays, which we located, and after twenty minutes, the creatures were all dead.

Around the same time, we invited one of my husband's soldier friends to spend the weekend with us. He was looking forward to some time away from the barracks and, most of all, some decent food. After a pleasant evening, we decided to get an early night. At 5 A.M., I opened the door to use the bathroom and saw him sitting fully dressed in the lounge, his small bag by his side. He looked tired and said, "I've had a dreadful night in that bedroom; there's something very evil in there. Whatever it was, it tried to smother me and sat on my chest." I was so young, only seventeen, and didn't know what to say, especially when he said he was returning to the barracks. He thanked me for the hospitality and left hurriedly in his car. Over the next year, more soldier friends came to stay, but none would remain in the spare bedroom for long, and as most were unnerved, they usually beat a hasty retreat back to camp.

One day we were looking at some photos of me seated outside in a deck chair with my back next to our open bedroom window; we both gasped as we saw the grinning face of a man leering at us. As the situation steadily worsened, we packed up our things and found a new place to live.

THE INTERACTIVE PERSONALITY GHOST

INTERACTIVE GHOSTS ARE THE MOST prevalent type and can move, communicate, and occasionally address the living. They are usually those of a departed person or a family member. Depending on their personality when they were alive, they can be either kind or hostile, and can physically touch the living. It is not uncommon for this spirit to walk around and create sounds; some will even leave their handprints on glass, mirrors, or tables. Others may emit an odor, such as perfume or cigar smoke, to notify you of their presence. Experts believe this ghost type retains its previous identity and may still hold on to its emotions. They usually come to comfort you or to notify you of something important.

THE FUNNEL GHOST

THE FUNNEL GHOST IS NONAGGRESSIVE and will haunt houses or ancient historic structures, so the buildings may have cold spots when one of these spirits is in situ. Most paranormal specialists believe they are a loved one returning for a visit, or possibly a past occupant of the property. They can be seen taking the shape of a spinning funnel and are frequently captured in pictures or on film as a faint transparent apparition or a whirling spiral of light.

THE ECTOPLASM OR ECTO-MIST

ACCORDING TO EXPERTS, AN ECTO-MIST or ghostly mist is a vaporous cloud typically appearing several feet above the ground. It can move quickly or remain stationary, almost as if circling. These ghostly apparitions, whether white, gray, or even black, have been documented in several films and images. They have been known to emerge as ectoplasms before transforming into full-bodied apparitions. Many people have seen them at cemeteries, battlefields, and historical sites.

SHADOW PEOPLE
OR SHADOW MEN

SHADOW PEOPLE ARE BLACK SEMITRANSPARENT figures sometimes reaching over six feet in height or appearing as small as a child. These entities can take on a humanoid form and dwell in the corners of a room. It's common to see them in your peripheral vision as a black cloud, and they are known to move quickly, with a swirling fog. People describe them as being faceless, sometimes having glowing red eyes. These beings have been reported for thousands of years and in various civilizations. Still, no one knows if they are malevolent spirits, time-traveling entities from another dimension, or even aliens. One idea holds that they are imprisoned souls caught in a limbo-like state, unable to reach the light, while others say that they do not behave like ghosts and are much more sinister, and comparable to demons.

The alien notion may appear farfetched, but it is not as ridiculous as it seems since many individuals who encounter these entities believe they were abducted shortly after seeing one. Those unfortunate enough to encounter a shadow man tell of how they feel complete paralysis engulf their body, and however hard they try, they cannot move a muscle; this is followed by a heaviness on the recipient's chest until they can no longer breathe. The personality of this entity is menacing and, like similar demonic beings, feeds on the fear of the living. In the last ten years, reports of this creature have increased, and there is a lot of coverage of them on YouTube and paranormal TV shows. Apart from sitting on the chests of its victims, it can also choke its prey and roughly drag them out of bed by their feet; this might leave bruises or long scratches on a person's body. They also focus on innocent babies and small children and can slide under bedsheets or lie in wait under beds. Shadow men dash from room to room, peeking behind doorways and suddenly appearing to people in hallways and staircases to block access. They can cause disruptions within a home for many years, creating mental breakdowns and despair. If they are interdimensional beings, eliminating them would not seem very easy because of their cunning and advanced knowledge.

Science will quickly label it as a sort of sleep paralysis, which might very well be the case.

CASE STUDY: ZACHARY,
TOLD BY HIS MOTHER, FERN

Since birth, my beautiful blond-haired son, Zachary, experienced the worst night terrors. He hated going to sleep and would fuss at bedtime. Things became so bad that we would drive him around in the car every evening, hoping he might fall asleep.

At eleven months old, Zachary was sitting in his high chair and happily babbling away when he suddenly froze, staring through me, and then out of nowhere, he let out an ear-piercing scream. He refused to look at my face, and no matter how hard I tried, I couldn't console him. From then on, these kinds of outbursts started to happen frequently.

Zachary, a very gentle, psychic child, stopped to look at trees and flowers and empathized with older people; he treated them with great respect. He was particularly fond of animals and had a strange connection with them. Once when we were just about to get in the car, a cat sat down in front of him. He stared at it for a while and then said, "Mummy, he's just told me he's been lost for six months and is very hungry." Suddenly, a car screeched to a halt, and a woman jumped out of the vehicle and grabbed the cat. "At last, we've found him," she said, "he's been missing for six months!"

Being an early talker, at age two, he shocked me when he started mentioning an alien invasion. We were perplexed about how he would know about aliens as we had never talked about them or watched any TV shows that portrayed them. I asked when this invasion would happen; he replied, "Maybe today, maybe tomorrow." He then went on to tell me that spaceships were on Earth now, most of them under the ocean.

When he was four, we were out walking when he said casually, "Mummy, those two people that have just passed us are aliens; there are lots of them here now." He constantly speaks about when the zombies or aliens make themselves visible to everyone and says we must leave ahead of time. He even has a bag packed and ready!

It became evident that Zachary was psychic. One day he told me that his grandmother would die; sure enough, a week later, we sadly lost her. He then started to name people who had previously lived in our house. We had no clue as to who used to live in our home, but he was reeling off names so freely. We decided to research these names; again, every-thing he said was correct. One day he casually remarked that his teenage sister had started smoking. After I remonstrated with her, she started crying and said she had been doing this after school with her friends.

Things took a sinister turn as Zachary started to be tor-mented by an evil spirit. He called him "the mean man" or "Woe" and said he wore all-black clothes with long sleeves and a hood. This creature would dash from room to room, following Zachary everywhere he went. A few weeks later, Zachary insisted on wearing all black and nagged me for a black hoodie, which Woe had told him to wear. After a while, he was so disturbed by this creature that he wouldn't leave my side. If I went to the bathroom, he would curl up outside the door in the fetal position until I came out. He had to have one of us stay with him at bedtime until he fell asleep, then he would wake with dreadful night terrors; it broke my heart to see him so tormented.

And so, as a desperate mother, I contacted Beleta and asked her if she knew of any way to help him. Beleta supposed that Woe was a shadow person, known to try to steal a per-son's light to gain superior power. She immediately contacted around sixty people on Facebook to ask that they send him encouraging affirmations of protection. Many of the healers said prayers for Zachary; some lit candles, and others just sent well-wishes, which all seemed to help because, within a month, he was transformed. He now sleeps peacefully at night, has no fears of Woe or being alone, and refuses to talk about him. I hope he has retained some of his psychic abilities,

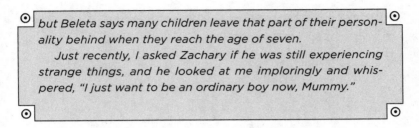

but Beleta says many children leave that part of their personality behind when they reach the age of seven.

Just recently, I asked Zachary if he was still experiencing strange things, and he looked at me imploringly and whispered, "I just want to be an ordinary boy now, Mummy."

If a family home is being haunted by any kind of demon or ghost, the family members have to be mindful of the younger generation and to remember they are very naive, much like a sponge that can absorb atmospheres of either good or bad. Conversations about the haunting are best had out of the earshot of little children, because any kind of paranormal horrors that are present in life might be enough to affect the child's confidence or have a lasting effect on their personality.

PROTECTION

AN EFFECTIVE way of getting rid of demonic energies that cling to people is to use the strongest expletives and direct them with full force to fight back at them. Also summon Archangel Michael daily through prayer and wear black obsidian, black tourmaline, and fluorite all the time; these crystals will put up a protective barrier. For more information on protective crystals, see page 172. If the demon still refuses to leave, seeking the help of a priest is essential. Demons hate any reference to God or religion, so whatever your faith, usually, a religious leader can move them on. If children have been targeted like Zachary above, consider getting them baptized again or dab them daily with holy water. If you're religious, you could leave an open Bible in the room or entreat Jesus to help with the situation. An ordained minister or a paranormal investigator could also devise different methods to disperse this problem.

POLTERGEISTS

POLTERGEISTS ARE NOISY AND DISRUPTIVE and are especially attracted to teenagers, leaving some theorists to suggest that rather than the ghost being a living entity, poltergeists are more of an unruly energy that the young individual creates. No one can really prove this either way, but what is clear is that these kinds of hauntings are probably the worst of all. Poltergeists throw things across the room, open cupboards and slam doors, make loud noises, and attack by biting, scratching, pushing, and pulling. Like other demonic spirits, they feed on a person's fear and gain strength from frightening people. Poltergeists are hard to eliminate, and often a priest will be brought in to cleanse a person or a property.

CASE STUDY: LEANNA
PETRIFYING POLTERGEIST

Years ago, when I was around eighteen, I worked as a cook in a nursing home and met a sixteen-year-old girl who was quite gawky and socially awkward. We'll call her Sarah. She didn't speak to anyone much and kept to herself. A few nurses were in the kitchen talking about ghosts and spirits, and I told them about a haunted cottage I used to live in.

When they all dispersed and went about their business, Sarah returned to my empty kitchen and asked if she could talk to me. Of course I said yes, and listened while she told me she had a poltergeist in her house. She said her mother had asked her to clean the kitchen, and when she had finished and left the room, seconds later, her mother had reprimanded her. Not knowing why, Sarah returned to the kitchen, only to find all the cupboard doors and drawers were wide open, and the dining chairs were all positioned on top of the table.

She then said the same night, she was lying on the couch, eating an orange, and she placed the peel on the floor. When she reached down to clear the peel away, she said it was frozen. She was clearly upset and very frightened, so I tried to help by telling her to summon her guardian angel so they could protect her. I wasn't sure I believed her tale and thought nothing more of it until the following day.

The nurses stood in a long line, all carrying dinner trays so I could serve breakfast to the residents. Sarah was amongst the crowd when suddenly, a coffee mug slithered down the countertop and smashed into the wall right next to me. Everyone saw it, and most fled the room. Sarah, looking shaken, said, "That was because of me, wasn't it?" After witnessing that, I had no choice but to believe her, so I spent a lot of time over the coming days to try to figure out ways of sending this entity away. I told her to purchase a white sage smudging stick, light it, and wave the smoke in every room of the house. I then went into more depth about summoning angels and suggested she meditate at night, visualizing herself in a golden bubble.

A few nights later, I was settling down to sleep when I got this very uneasy feeling. Suddenly, I heard what I could only describe as snorting coming from the bottom of my bed.

> *I quickly put the light on, and there was nothing amiss, so I turned it off and put it down to my imagination. Moments later, I was slapped hard over my cheek, and when my eyes sprang open, I saw two dark, beady eyes inches from my face. This creature looked to be half animal, half human, with a long brown snout. It turned away, snorted, and walked up and down the room for most of the night. I was completely paralyzed with fear and couldn't even yell for help. I psychically knew that whatever this creature was, it was angry with me because I had given Sarah the tools to rid herself of him once and for all. Thankfully, it only visited me once because my mother stepped in and banished it.*

PROTECTION

THIS PRACTICE can be performed to rid the home of any kind of spirit and is very effective.*

Sage has been used throughout the ages to cleanse and remove any evil spirits or energy left behind. Most of the time, white sage is burnt in a bundle called a smudging stick, which can be purchased relatively cheaply online, and this is okay if you want to sanitize an area. Many people don't realize that to remove entities or ghosts, you need more than just a few smoky trails of the herb to succeed.

White sage is thought to be the most effective, but you can use any variety of sage as long as there is a lot of it, and it is properly dried.

To rid my bedroom of this creature, Mother made sure she

---

* Note: We cannot stress enough how dangerous it is to work with fire magic, so make sure you have a fire extinguisher nearby and ensure all children and pets are removed from the home before commencing.

wore a face mask and filled a sizeable fireproof bowl with two cups of dried sage; she then lit it, and once it burned nicely, she blew out the flames. Making sure all the windows in the house were closed, she walked into every room and even the understairs cubbyhole and filled them all with sage smoke. In each room, she recited the following words: *"Entity be gone; we shall have none."* And then she closed the door. The final room she cleansed was the kitchen, and to extinguish the flames, she submerged the bowl of smoking herbs in water. We then left the house for around five hours, and when we returned, she opened all the doors and windows to let out any leftover spirits.

ANIMAL GHOSTS

ON A LIGHTER NOTE, ANIMAL ghosts are significantly less common than human ghosts. They frequently remain where they feel most comfortable, such as close to the bed or their feeding location. They typically haunt the areas where they lived rather than where they died, but they can also enter a person's dream, perhaps to connect with their owner. When we share our life with an animal, we create a bond, and often the pet will wait until its owner passes away before it can finally leave the earthly plane.

SUPERNATURAL CREATURES

DEMONS

DEMONS ARE EVIL SUPERNATURAL BEINGS that are significant in literature, fiction, mythology, and folklore. One mustn't assume they are akin to regular spirits because unlike ghosts, demons are nonhuman and reside in a different dimension; they are also cunning and capable of imitating benign spirits. For some reason, demons are particularly visible to children, probably because infants are psychic up until about the age of seven or eight. They can frequently assume the form of another child or an imaginary friend, so it is very challenging to tell whether a demon has taken up residence in your home or if it's just a friendly ghost. These creatures are all-powerful and can wreck lives, and it's unlikely that the usual methods used to rid a home of entities will work.

If you think you have one, it could be time to get some professional help from a priest or a medium and have the entity properly removed with prayer and ritual.

DEMONIC POSSESSION:
HOW TO TELL IF SOMEONE IS POSSESSED

AS WE'VE learned in a previous chapter, these beings can enter the bodies of weak or susceptible people and take control of their minds. There are many telltale signs that a demon is possessing someone, so the following are guidelines that can help determine whether this is the case or not. Of course, a person's behavior could have nothing to do with a demonic walk-in at all.

- The victim could show signs of having suppressed emotions like anger and resentment; they might also be argumentative, and unkind to family members. Sometimes, they can rant or be physically abusive.
- Animals or family pets will notice immediately that something is amiss and may bark at the person or run away and hide.
- Over time, the victim may lose their appetite or stop eating and lose drastic amounts of weight. Appearing visibly different, their face will alter or become contorted when they speak.
- A more noticeable way you can tell if a demon is possessing someone is when they speak through their victim. The voice will not be their own and will perhaps sound deeper or resemble a growl.
- Foul language might be displayed, followed by disturbing laughter.
- Objects might fly around the room, or the victim might give off a strange smell.
- The target might become physically stronger, showing signs of superhuman strength.
- The person may experience deep depression, have no motivation, or even feel suicidal.
- After being healthy, the victim's health could suddenly decline.
- The target can begin levitating, suspended in the air for short periods of time, or furniture around the possessed individual may rise upward. Sometimes, a bed might shake or rise and fall.

- Often a victim may begin to choke or vomit a black mucus.
- The victim may stare into space for a long period of time, or appear detached from their body.
- When someone is completely possessed by a spirit, they may demonstrate dangerous behavior, like venturing outside alone, in the middle of the night.

People also tell of swarms of ants and other insects or even the presence of a snake or a single black bird, like a crow or a raven, who might try to enter the house.

PROTECTION

DEMONIC POSSESSION is traumatic for the victim and their loved ones, who have no choice but to sit back hopelessly and watch. Usual methods of smudging with sage or other such rituals rarely work because the entity is too powerful. Some mediums can cast out a demon, but these cases are uncommon. A religious minister is usually employed to carry out an exorcism consisting of several prayers spoken over the possessed individual. Often, things will get worse before they get better, with some exorcisms being very volatile.

CASE STUDY: ROLAND DOE

Many people have seen the disturbing film The Exorcist, *which shows a female child being possessed by a demon. The movie was based on the true account of Roland Doe, a thirteen-year-old boy who lived in Washington, DC, in the late 1940s. He was haunted by a demonic ghost for a year after using a Ouija board. The child had scratches on his body and would vomit, and use profanity. His bed shook, unusual dripping noises could be heard, and writing would appear on the bedroom wall. His visits to psychiatrists, doctors, and mediums were ineffective.*

The family permitted to have him exorcised by two Catholic priests, which caused the young boy to be very disturbed and tormented. During the ritual, suddenly, a deep voice came from within the child and said, "Satan, Satan, I am Saint Michael. I command you, Satan and other evil spirits, to leave this body. In the name of Dominus, now! Now! Now!" Weakly, Roland said, "He is gone now." Afterward, he remarked that he had seen the fiery sword of the Archangel Michael. After this spiritual cleansing, Roland returned to being physically and mentally healthy.

Helpful information can come from spiritual churches, or a reputable medium can put one in touch with the right source. Often a house blessing will have to be done, too, to offer protection for all who live there.

A PRAYER TO ARCHANGEL MICHAEL

IF YOU are faced with something demonic and you're alone or frightened, reciting the Lord's Prayer repeatedly often works. You can also ask Archangel Michael to protect you and surround you with light.

Speak this short mantra over and over again:

"Angel Michael, keep me safe, be by my side, and guard my space."

JINN-DJINN

WE HAVE all heard of the genie and the magic lamp, represented in films such as *Aladdin*. Still, in Islamic tradition, "jinn" is used to collectively describe supernatural creatures. Most Arabic regions and Islamic traditions feature stories about the jinn, but similar beings can also be found in other cultures' customs and traditions.

Some jinn, like demons, are evil and can possess humans or absorb their energy, while in other tales, they are depicted as more benevolent spirits. The jinn are believed to exist in the spectral realm and can cross over to the Earth plane if summoned. They are generally invisible but can shapeshift, appearing as black dogs or snakes, and are thought to be the spreaders of mental illness and disease. It is not unusual for these creatures to possess someone, but conditions must be right before they can achieve this. Suppose a person shows violent bouts of anger, excessive fear, extreme heedlessness, or is overly focused on themselves. In that case, they are vulnerable to psychic attacks and can find themselves sharing their body with the jinn. If possessed by this creature, they might experience seizures, loss of appetite, sadness, anxiety, or bouts of anger.

Like with any spirit possession, an exorcism might have to be performed.

INCUBUS (MALE) AND SUCCUBUS (FEMALE)

THESE DEMONS have a complex past and are said to have a life-span of 150 to 200 years. They typically have great charisma and incredible stamina and appear physically attractive, with wings, a long tail, and horns. The uglier troll-type incubi are less common. According to legend, the incubus and succubus were originally angels in heaven who helped Lucifer revolt against God and, after that, became "fallen angels." Incubi are frequently portrayed as nighttime lovers who paralyze and rape their victims by placing a heaviness on their chest so they cannot move. Their attacks can occur in the cold light of day or, more often, in disturbing dreams; sometimes, the rapes can happen regularly and last for many years. They show no respect and can also be physically abusive, leaving scratches or bruises on the victim's body. If someone moves house to escape the assaults, the entity has been known to follow them from property to property, sometimes attacking them regularly for as long as twenty years.

CASE STUDY: MARY
SINISTER SEX

My story is one I have rarely spoken about, mainly because I am still traumatized by the event. A relative of mine had inherited a small apartment in London, previously owned by her husband's brother, who had passed away. Knowing I was exhausted from work, she offered the flat to me for a week's vacation. As soon as I entered the property, I sensed an intense heaviness in the air, especially when I approached the bedroom. Immediately, I thought someone was watching me, but I brushed off the feeling and settled down for the night. I had no trouble drifting to sleep, but at around 1 A.M., I swiftly jackknifed into a sitting position when a phantom figure crawled into the bed beside me. Suddenly, I was forcefully flipped over and pinned facedown onto the bed by an unidentified hand, who then engaged me in vulgar acts of anal sex. My ordeal lasted several minutes, and I was shivering in terror once it was over. I quickly gathered my possessions and fled the building. It took me three years of counseling and a brief stay in a mental health facility before I could begin moving on from the encounter. I sought the help of a spiritual healer, who advised me to wear protective crystals to fend off any further attacks, and after a little while, some of my confidence returned. I eventually told my relative why I cut my vacation short and warned her against going into the property. She and her husband immediately put the apartment up for sale.

PROTECTION

AS THE incubi have no respect for religion, it can be difficult to eliminate them as they tend to be unaffected by priests, holy water, and exorcisms. Moving house could solve the problem, but incubi have been known to attach themselves to people and follow them wherever they go. The best solution is to contact a paranormal investigator who works closely with mediums to dispel the entity. Another more profound method of protecting yourself against an incubus is to summon the violet flame.

THE VIOLET FLAME OF SAINT-GERMAIN

Other names: the Flame of Transmutation, Flame of Mercy, Flame of Freedom

THE VIOLET flame has its connection to Count Saint Germain (an ascended master) and epitomizes the essence of perfection. It seldom appears in books for protection against psychic attack, which is surprising because it is a powerful tool against anything demonic or supernatural. It appears as a violet light that heals and purifies a person or environment with its colorful hues. The knack is implementing its power, but this can be accomplished with practice.

If a person witnesses the miracle of this phenomenon, they are said to be on the higher echelons of spiritual advancement. Its powers of protection are so exorbitant it is believed to aid every problem known to humankind: health, mental healing, fear, phobias, depression, lack of self-esteem, etc. It also clears karmic blockages and is said to purify negativity.

Learning how to meditate is a must to gain access to the violet flame's power. First, find a peaceful place to begin. Sitting upright in a comfortable chair, close your eyes and place your palms upward, resting on your lap. Focus on the third-eye chakra, which is situated between the eyebrows. Practice looking through this, taking your time not to rush, because hopefully, this is where the violet color will start to emerge. Recite this mantra seven times to focus the mind:

"Violet light with flame so bright.
Protect my soul both day and night.
Shine down your power this earthly hour.
Shield my being and fight my plight."

If you see the flame behind your closed eyes or any violet light, ask it directly to protect you. Even if you don't see it, the mantra is sometimes enough to summon the flame, which will later help you with your problem. Afterward, you will notice a distinct change in your home's energy and any dark vibrations will be gone.

CASE STUDY: LEANNA
VIOLET LIGHTS

Since learning about the violet flame, for many years, I would repeatedly practice looking out through my third-eye chakra in the hope of being able to see it. Only after a few years of practicing did I catch my first glimpse.

Two unkind women had targeted me at work, and they delighted in saying unpleasant comments about my appearance. When they learned about my Wiccan faith, their laughs and jeers were replaced with a barrage of more hostile comments, accusing me of being in league with Satan, and every time one of them walked past me, they would whisper "Devil worshipper" under their breath. Of course, if you know anything about witchcraft today, you will understand that witches don't believe in the devil because it's a Christian concept; nevertheless, it was all becoming too much, and after being at such a low ebb, I seriously considered leaving my job and looking for something else. Suddenly, the bullies turned their attention to another young girl at work. She was gentle but had a weight problem, and they would delight in calling her a "fat cow." One day, I caught her crying in the staff room, so after finally having enough of their relentless tormenting, I reported the women to my line manager. She appeared to listen and showed sympathy, but even after hearing about the abuse, she dismissed it and told me not to be so sensitive. Things got so bad that my gentle colleague left her position, and once again, I was the target. I couldn't understand why these women were so unpleasant, but every day, a new torrent of abuse awaited me. During one incident, they cornered me in the stock room, and one even jostled me when I was trying to leave the bathroom. This time I wrote a letter to the company's director, explaining how our line manager had simply swept the matter under the rug and that if something wasn't done about it, I would also be looking for alternative employment.

After having had a terrible day with one of the women, hoping for some comfort, I decided to meditate and connect to a higher source. After twenty minutes of controlled breathing, I saw some activity through my third-eye chakra. Far in the distance, there was a tiny lavender orb, no bigger than the tip of my finger, and it was bouncing about; suddenly, it merged with another and another until there were hundreds of them. The colors were bright violet and pink, swirling and dancing behind my closed eyes; they were breathtakingly beautiful. I began to feel the physical effects of the light when my entire body started to buzz. It was all-consuming and filled every inch of me with love and total understanding of who I was. I remained in this beautiful space for about five minutes, all the time in my mind asking the light to help me banish the negativity around me and to distance myself from the bullies.

Two days later, the company's director called me into his office and offered me a promotion. He had sacked the line manager and offered me her position. It was more money, but better still, I was now in charge of heading the team, meaning the obnoxious women were now answerable to me. I couldn't risk anyone else going through a similar experience, so after thinking long and hard about it, I decided to sack them both. A miracle happened thanks to the violet flame, and just like I had asked, all negativities left my life.

BANSHEES

THIS CREATURE is based on ancient Irish legends and is shown as an older woman with long gray hair. Her mouth is constantly open because she enjoys torturing the living with her relentless, piercing scream, and it is said that when she connects with her victim, she can shatter glass or rupture eardrums. These spirits can stalk their prey to attack or harm. Some people think that a banshee visit is related to death and that she will arrive when someone close to the victim is going to die. Because of her hellish sobbing, her eyes are perpetually red, and those who encounter her regularly can go insane.

DOPPELGÄNGER

DOPPELGÄNGERS, A sort of ghost from Northern Europe, are said to mimic a person's appearance, and although frequently linked to German folklore, they are a regular occurrence in all cultures. Some legends tell you that if you see your doppelgänger, bad luck will follow, possibly resulting in death. There are methods for banishing the negative karma that a doppelgänger brings. These include removing your clothing right away, flipping it inside out, and putting it back on. Another strategy is to bathe immediately, to wash the bad luck away.

SPIRIT VAMPIRES

SLAVIC CULTURE gave rise to this kind of ghostly looking creature. Every nation, from Russia and Ukraine to Scotland, Ireland, and Greece, has its own take on the vampire. These creatures need to feed on human blood to survive and can even walk amongst the living. They might stand out in a crowd as their bodies exhibit signs of their unnatural nature, such as pale, ill-looking skin and lack of heartbeat. Although we don't report many sightings of vampires anymore, these creatures are considered interdimensional. When a portal opens, the vampire can enter the earthly realm and create havoc.

WRAITH

THE TERM "wraith" is a Scottish word to describe spirits and ghosts. In medieval times wraiths could allegedly mimic a human and torment them mercilessly until they either went insane or committed suicide. In some European countries, the wraith was believed to be the soul of a vengeful, dead mortal who had unfinished business and would return to life to take revenge. They are skeletal figures covered in ragged black clothing and discovered in abandoned locations like dungeons and cemeteries. These undead spirits are 100 percent evil and infused with negative energy; they will prey on their victims and revel in their distress. Like other forms of evil spirits, they gain their strength from the fear and suffering of others, so when they attach themselves to someone, the person might go downhill fast.

If the wraith is around any form of plant or foliage, it will wither and die.

PROTECTION

SUNLIGHT REPELS the wraith, so inviting light into your life is a way to rid yourself of one. At night when you have no choice but to be in the dark, before going to sleep, visualize yourself in a bright white light and imagine yourself encompassed in a heavenly glow. If this doesn't work, burn red sage in the bedroom. As above, see page 148 for more information on dragon's blood. Remember, however frightened you might feel, try to be courageous and show no fear.

Part III

CURSES & BLACK MAGIC

ENERGY IS SIMPLY ENERGY; IT'S neither good nor bad. Like electricity, it constantly flows around us and can morph into either a negative or a positive vibe. Most practicing witches today work closely with nature and will only perform spells with good intent. It's a known fact that witchcraft comes with specific guidelines, one of which is to "harm none" nor to influence the mindset of others. Everyone is said to have free will when they arrive on Earth; therefore, using magic to change someone's perspective is seen to interfere with their karma. When casting spells, it can be difficult to determine where the ethical line lies between what is acceptable and what is not. For instance, you cannot perform a spell to win the heart of someone you are madly in love with because that would influence a person's free will. You can, however, use a spell to attract the person's attention; this way, it will be their choice whether they want to pursue a relationship with you.

On the other hand, black magic is more commonly practiced in secret and is usually performed by people working alone. Those who participate in the dark arts can access and manipulate this energy force to their advantage. Practitioners don't exercise the same disciplines as those working for the greater good and will think nothing of meddling in a person's life, upsetting the karmic balance.

Emotions generate any form of magical energy, so, for example, if your neighbor is continually complaining, you can take all the proper steps to follow the guidelines and cast a spell to quieten them for a while. Still, if you are internally furious and spitting feathers, your negative energy will eventually reach them. Because of this, many witches worldwide believe it's crucial to remove the emotion when performing magic and never to cast a spell when you're in the wrong frame of mind.

CURSES

CURSES OR HEXES ARE MORE often than not associated with magical spells and are directed at a person to cause them harm in some way. These deliberate acts of evil intent can vary, from causing emotional stress to physical illness and, in extreme cases, even death. Like with the evil eye, casting a curse on someone is relatively easy and can be manifested by simply wishing the person harm. As with most magical practices, it is believed that the bounce-back effect might occur if you knowingly curse someone; this happens when the harmful intent fails to reach its target, gaining more momentum along the way, thus, bouncing back to the sender. Of course, no scientific proof exists that curses or hexes are real. Still, we know that every action we project in life, from physically touching something to speaking, gives off energy. If you're in the vicinity of negativity, it could affect you.

Another theory is that curses only work if you believe in them and that if you feel something awful will happen to you, you may add to the power and cause it to happen. For us, this is a gray area. We are both retired Tarot readers, and when we were seeing clients regularly, often a person would come for a reading who was suffering a great deal of bad luck and misfortune. It wasn't until we delved into the cards that we discovered they had an enemy, and this individual wished them great harm. The customer had no clue they were on the receiving end of a curse, yet their life was still spiraling out of control.

CASE STUDY: LEANNA
THE GREENAWAY CURSE

Some years ago, before my mother retired from her Tarot readings, she had unintentionally upset one of her customers when she relayed information the client didn't want to hear. This situation can sometimes happen when people visit psychics, and there is no way of knowing how someone will receive the information you give them. The client had gone home and told her adult son all about it, who then contacted my mother online. It was a vile email, stating very clearly that he had cursed her and that she would fall over and hurt her leg, resulting in her inability to walk. Even Mum, who was familiar with curses and knew how to counteract them, felt vulnerable. It worried her, and naturally, she spent a few weeks being quite upset about it. I kept telling her the curse wouldn't be active if she failed to believe it, but it still played on her mind. Having spent most of my adult life practicing witchcraft, I immediately took matters into my own hands and began a series of protection rituals. I intended to surround her in a protective light and send the curse back to the sender, but to do this, I had to draw on more power than I ever had before. I knew I was supposed to be careful and not get too angry while casting these spells because, as we have just mentioned, magic can intensify when someone is in a heightened state of emotion, and believe me, I was emotional! I was so furious with the man for sending this negativity to my mother that I emailed him back and told him in no uncertain terms that he had picked on the wrong witch. To mimic his curse, I made it very clear that should anything untoward happen to her, the same fate would befall him threefold. I don't know if this affected him because we never heard

> *from him again, but despite my relentless counter spells, not long after, Mum did indeed hurt her foot so severely she couldn't walk properly for nearly a year. Sometimes, even the most well-schooled witches can't undo a curse!*

HOODOO, ROOT WORK, CONJUROR

HOODOO WAS FIRST INTRODUCED BY African American enslaved peoples and is not to be confused with voodoo. It was born of the need for power, justice, and protection from the predators who enslaved them. They performed hoodoo spells and rituals to gain some form of control and protection in their lives. Hence, they were able to create a balance of power against daily beatings, starvation, and sexual abuse, thus restoring self-esteem and a more peaceful existence. The spells varied in strength and type, with some reporting to be aggressive and vengeful, especially toward their enslavers, while others were more benign, creating love potions or perhaps healing spells for the sick. Many conjurors were mindful of watching their karma, but others would cast caution to the wind and cause sickness and evil to the wrongdoers. The spells held simple ingredients such as spices, herbs, and salt, and often Tarot cards and candles would be included, along with personal items belonging to the perpetrators. An enslaved person might wear a little mojo filled with protective herbs and spice, with tiny crystals and a pinch of graveyard dirt as a magical defense. The mojos would be worn around the neck for a week to ensure protection.

Hoodoo spells often incorporated recitations of the Psalms as the enslaved people had varying religious beliefs, which they hoped would help them find the source of their own power.

Today hoodoo priests and witches primarily work on the side of good, but as with any faith, there are always those who explore and implement the darker sides.

Suppose you get on the wrong side of someone who practices the dark arts. In that case, hoodoo magic is potent, so the victim might expect regular visits from demons and monsters or smaller entities that follow the person around their whole life.

CURSED OBJECTS

CURSING A SMALL ITEM SUCH as a pebble, charm, trinket, book, or something that can go unnoticed is an efficient technique to wreak havoc in a person's life. It's not necessary for the targeted person to physically own the item, either. Dark practitioners will perform a ritual to anchor evil or demonic energy to an object before slipping it into your home or perhaps your place of employment. In some cases, objects can remain undetected for decades, generating a stream of bad luck that can affect a person or residence if they are not discovered. It is not unusual for an older property to have an ancient, cursed object somewhere inside, especially if it dates back a few centuries. An amulet might be hidden under floorboards or placed discreetly inside a fireplace; sometimes, it can even be cemented into the bricks of a home to avoid being found.

Sometimes, you might encounter a strange object that isn't intended to hinder or harm you. People in the past were superstitious and would also place certain items in the home to bless the property, ward off witches, and bring good luck. In England, the builders of a house would often put playing cards under the floorboards to bring peace and good fortune, press coins into the wet cement of the foundations for prosperity, and in older buildings, dating back as far as the thirteenth century, a single shoe might be placed in the walls of the home to repel dark and evil influences. Nobody is sure why they decided to embed shoes in the walls. One theory is that shoes are the only item of clothing that takes the shape of the human who wears them and that they somehow capture the wearer's essence, which gives them the ultimate power of protection. The shoes often belonged to children, probably because footwear was expensive in ancient times, so they recycled them. They have also been found in strange places like inside chimneys, attics, and even under the floorboards.

PROTECTION

FINDING AN ancient, cursed object in your home shouldn't affect you directly because it was probably created to harm someone who is no longer there or alive. However, if the item was designed to wreak havoc in the home, any lingering energy could still be present. If you come across any object that looks sinister or unfamiliar anywhere in your house, the best cause of action is to get rid of it. If it's made from a burnable material, set fire to it outside or take it far away from the property and bury it in the ground. Once the object has been destroyed, peace should follow. If you are lucky enough to discover a shoe, it should be safe to leave it in place.

HAUNTED OBJECTS

ALTHOUGH RARE, HAUNTED OBJECTS DO exist. There are museums dedicated to these items in many locations across the world. A spirit can attach itself to any artifact, such as dolls, furniture, works of art, and even something small like scissors.

However, if you move house to avoid a ghost, and the item travels with you, you will continue to be haunted. The same can be said if the object changes hands or ends up in a different house or country; the spirit will trail it wherever it goes.

Ghosts will attach themselves to things if some sentimentality is associated. Perhaps the previous owner led an unhappy life or has unfinished business.

The Great Bed of Ware, allegedly built for King Edward IV in the fifteenth century, is considered a haunted object. The bed is beautifully carved and spent decades being housed in different Ware inns. During this time, commoners who slept in the bed throughout the years covered it in graffiti and destroyed the delicate woodwork, leaving the frame beaten and weathered. According to folklore, the bed's maker, carpenter Jonas Fosbrooke, was so furious by the disrespectful handling of his work that his spirit attacked any commoner who tried to lie in it. The bed is presently on show at the Victoria and Albert Museum in London.

CASE STUDY: TRUDI
THE HAUNTED PANEL

I've always loved ancient things and have collected several items over the years. I was living and working in Italy when I was drawn toward an antique shop down one of the side streets. Standing before me was a huge Indian wall panel ornately carved in wood and decorated with bone. It took my breath away when I saw it. It stood around six feet tall and was so detailed with intricate craftsmanship. I just had to buy it. The shop owner told me she had two wall panels; another that she housed elsewhere was slightly different but just as beautiful as the one in the shop. She asked if I would like to see it. My heart was set on this one, so I refused, and she continued to tell me how lovely the other one was and even invited me to her home to view it. She lived a fair distance from the store, and I was due to fly back to the UK the next day, so I declined her offer again.

Back in England, I was in the process of moving house, so when the panel finally arrived, without unpacking it, I put it straight into storage. By the time I had moved in, had some restoration work done, and then redecorated, it was close to a year before I was ready to unveil my treasure. To my horror, when I finally opened the large wooden box, the wall panel was completely different from the one I had picked out in the store. I remembered how the store owner had said she had two and how she had tried so desperately to sell me the other. She must have switched them, I thought. I went to great lengths to contact the store owner, but after a year, it seemed she had packed up and moved on. I was stuck with this antique now, and although it was as beautiful as she had described, something about it made me feel uneasy.

Strange things started to happen the moment I hung it on my living room wall. The window blinds would shake, and I began to have terrifying nightmares. I didn't make the connection straight away and thought as my house was old, it must be haunted. Cold spots started to appear in some of the rooms, and at times I could hear people whispering. One evening as I went to sleep, I had an out-of-body experience. I floated out of my body and traveled into the lounge, and there before me was the ghost of a little blond girl, about the age of nine, prettily dressed, with a bow around her waist and a bonnet on her head. She was standing beside my wall panel beckoning me to walk through it.

I followed her in, and immediately as I entered another room, I was pinned down on the floor by a revolting demon. I couldn't move or shout. As I looked up, five grotesque demons were all scampering across the ceiling. Their bodies were yellow and black with monstrous features, and the drool from their mouths slowly dripped onto my body. Suddenly, there was a loud bang, and I sat bolt upright in bed. The electricity had tripped out. I exited the bed, my heart still banging loudly, and walked outside to the fuse box. Once I flicked the switch, a feeling of doom engulfed me. I knew I had to return to my house and when I did, I stayed awake all night long.

A week later, a psychic friend came over for coffee, and she was immediately drawn to the panel. "That's a portal to a demonic realm," she said. I shuddered because I hadn't mentioned anything to her at all about my experience. When I finally told her how I had acquired it and the dream about the demons, she burnt sage and performed a ritual, hoping to close the portal. Sadly, her blessing failed to help, and whichever house I lived in, the same kind of paranormal activity would occur.

Over the years, I have repeatedly tried to sell the panel, but no one has ever wanted to buy it. It now sits in storage, awaiting its next owner.

CURSE JARS

THOSE WHO DABBLE IN DARK magic have one goal: to punish and disrupt their victim's life. One popular method is using curse jars, a glass vessel like a bottle or a mason jar. Inside they are packed with items such as pins, rusty nails, razor blades (or other kinds of sharp objects), urine, poisonous plants, and graveyard dirt. In ancient times, the vessel would be more of a stoneware jug or pot and would have worked in a similar way.

Witch bottles dating back to the seventeenth century have been found in old properties and studied by archaeologists. These were often created to counteract any spells and to serve as protection from witches and their black magic. They, too, would have sharp items inside and contain powerful herbs, bones, or thorns, and have been found placed in the eaves of houses, under the floorboards, inside the hearth, and even in riverbanks and graveyards.

PROTECTION

IF YOU stumble upon a jar of any sort sealed with objects inside, never touch it with your bare hands; wear some heavy-duty gloves. Put it outside, place it on top of some newspaper, and then break the jar into small pieces with a hammer. Gather all the contents, wrap them inside the newspaper, and dispose of them somewhere far away from the house.

Once the vessel is broken and removed, so is the curse.

POPPETS

A COMMON WAY TO CURSE someone is to use a poppet, a small hand-crafted doll around fifteen centimeters (six inches) in height, most commonly made with fabric. Inside are items such as a few strands of the victim's hair, finger- or toenail clippings, or a small object that belongs to the receiver. In some cases, it's not always necessary to use physical items belonging to the recipient because often, the caster's intent and mind power are so strong all it takes is the person's name written on a small piece of paper, folded up and placed inside the doll. Once the poppet has been created, a verbal incantation is spoken over the doll, while at the same time, the practitioner might insert pins into the fabric. Given the opportunity, the practitioner will hide the doll somewhere in the victim's home but more often than not, they will leave it placed on an altar of sorts where they can keep repeating the incantation as and when they feel like it.

It's often difficult to prove that someone has cast a hex on you. The signs are perhaps your life suddenly becomes very stressful. You may lose your job and fall ill with one ailment after another. Marriages might break down, or you could suffer a great financial loss. These problems in life may occur simultaneously, or it could be that the sufferer will experience one disaster in life after another without any reprieve. To feel suddenly depressed is one sign someone may have cursed you. You may unexpectedly drift into melancholy for no apparent reason or feel suicidal when there is nothing to trigger it. Also, the negative energy can swamp other members of the family, especially blood relatives or those closest to the victim. Of course, difficult situations can and do occur to people all the time, so just because you might have a run of bad luck doesn't necessarily mean you are cursed.

PROTECTION

THESE OBJECTS are rarely found, but like with curse jars, you mustn't touch them with your bare hands, so wear gloves. Often these dolls are made of fabric, so burning them is a sure way to break the curse. Wax effigies are also popular ways to make a poppet, so if you come across one of these, you need to melt it first and then bury the wax and any metal contents deep in the ground. Or, if you know the person who has cursed you, you can make a poppet of your own to counteract their magic.

CREATING A POPPET

TAKE A black piece of material and fold it in half. Cut out the shape of a person; it should measure around six inches (fifteen centimeters) in length. You should have two pieces of material that mirror each other. With red yarn or cotton (for strength), begin stitching the materials together, leaving a small opening on the head. Fill the doll with dried mugwort; this will protect you from any black magic. Write down the name of your enemy on a piece of paper. If you don't know them, write the words "those who curse me." Fold the paper three times and insert inside the poppet. Finally, close the doll by sewing the remaining material.

Wrap a few meters of thick red yarn or cord tightly around the doll. While you are doing this, say this incantation over and over until you run out of cord:

"I bind your feet so you cannot walk to me,
I bind your hands so you cannot reach out to me,
I bind your mouth so you cannot speak to me,
I bind your mind so you cannot think of me.
So mote it be."

When you have completed the spell, keep the doll nearby at all times; sleep with it beside your bed and carry it in your purse or pocket during the day. Within a week, the curse will be lifted. The poppet will continue to work if you keep it somewhere in the house, so afterward, put it somewhere safe and out of sight.

STARING AND SPEAKING

PLACING A HEX OR CURSE on someone can also be achieved by challenging your victim head-on. Intimidating someone by staring at them with evil intent and even indicating you have cursed them is enough to start the downward spiral of doom in their life. Words spoken aloud such as "I curse you!" or "I wish for you to rot in hell" and "From now on, everything will start to go wrong in your life" are just some ways to threaten and curse someone. Be warned, though, if the victim decides not to hand over their power to the perpetrator and point-blank refuses to acknowledge it, they indirectly put a shield of protection around themselves, which can cause the curse to backfire. There will be nowhere for the curse to go except back to the person who sent it.

PROTECTION

WEARING BLACK obsidian will always generate a shield around you that even the strongest of magic cannot penetrate. Twin this crystal with fluorite, amplifying the defense as fluorite transforms and neutralizes negative energy to positive. We both wear black obsidian daily, which also shields us from any unintentional ill will from others, like the evil eye. If a person curses you directly, say loudly and with force, "I send your curse back to you three-fold." This should dispel the hex immediately.

PHOTOGRAPH CURSES

IF SOMEONE WANTS TO CAST a spell on a person, either for a positive outcome or negative, photographs of the individual are a popular way to channel energy toward someone. These methods of cursing are highly effective because one can concentrate their energy on the face of a person. A dark practitioner might write their intention on the front or back of a photograph or scribble all over their victim's face using black ink.

CASE STUDY: BELETA
A BLACK MAGIC VOODOO CURSE

After living in Malaysia for two years, the army relocated my immediate family to Singapore. Soon after, my stepfather, a violent and abusive man, entered into an affair with a local woman who was a voodoo witch. At the age of seventeen, I decided to get out of the toxic environment and married Leanna's father in Serangoon. He was also a soldier and based in Malaysia. Shortly after our marriage, I developed the most unbearable pain in my right eye; the doctor and optician could find nothing wrong with it, but the dull pain persisted for a few years until we returned to England. We paid my mother and stepfather a visit, as they too had returned to the UK, and in the evening, they showed us some of the wedding photos we hadn't seen before. There was a lovely snapshot of us both, but when I inspected the image more closely, I noticed that someone had pierced a pinhole in my right eye. I stared in total disbelief and instinctively knew I had to rip up the picture and throw it onto the open fire. As I did this, the pain left me immediately. Later, my stepfather admitted that he had shown his mistress these pictures and supposed she had jinxed me out of spite because he'd ended their affair. Later, my mother told me my stepfather had come in from work one afternoon, dropped on all fours, and started barking like a dog. His voodoo mistress, it would seem, was very powerful. She had control of him, even from a different continent.

In the following years, my stepfather showed extreme behavioral changes with irrational bouts of violence. I can only assume the curse continued to the end of his sorry days.

PROTECTION

THE CRYSTAL selenite is all-powerful in cutting and removing bad energy that clings to a person. If you find a picture of yourself that has been tampered with in any way, burning it immediately is the most efficient way to break a curse. Afterward, it's advisable to do a cleansing ceremony on the subject to ensure that any residual negative energy is completely expelled. You will require assistance with this part. The targeted individual must stand with their legs slightly apart and arms out to the side. Take a piece of selenite at least fifteen centimeters long and sweep it around the person's entire body while getting as close to them as you can without touching them. Think about cutting and slicing the negative energy with each slash of the crystal, causing the energy to vanish.

MIND CONTROL

SOME CURSES ARE LESS PRACTICAL and involve conjuring a malevolent entity, such as a demon or monster, which is then directed toward the victim; this is very dark magic practiced by those who are adept at mind power. The person will summon these creatures through meditative practice or spell work using the upside-down image of a pentagram, a symbol drawn in blood, the bones of a black animal, and a selection of black candles. The incantation, which dates back centuries, is usually spoken in Latin. Once a demon has been conjured, it is programmed to visit the victim at night. The receiver may experience unsettled sleep, vulgar and disgusting nightmares, insomnia, or visits to the negative astral plane during dream sleep. If the sender is successful in their summoning, the creature can hang around the victim for months, gradually dragging them down until they lose all sight of what is good in their life.

CASE STUDY: JANET
A CONJURED DEMON

I've been a medium for over three decades and have seen countless clients and helped them connect to loved ones that have passed over. Many years ago, when I was dating my husband, Mike, we were part of a social group and frequented a club nearby. One night my friend's fiancé introduced us to an acquaintance of his called Richard. He was a very intense, dark-haired man in his late twenties with piercing green eyes. He was fascinated by Tarot cards, the Ouija board, and all things supernatural, and seemed to take a great deal of interest in me. Throughout the night, I caught him staring at me, which made me uncomfortable, to say the least, and then he began probing me about my psychic work and asked if I would consider joining forces to combine our skills. My psychic warning bells started to ring, and I knew I was in the presence of someone evil. I didn't want to be in the same room, let alone work, with him. In my mind, I silently asked my guides to show up and protect me, and thank goodness they did because we later found out he worshipped Satan. He was deeply immersed in the black arts and had a huge reversed pentagram painted on his bedroom floor.

A few days later, my friend called and was clearly upset. Because she knew I had some knowledge of ghosts, she described a situation she'd had the night before. A tall, shrouded creature loomed over her and stroked her face and breasts. This creature stayed beside her all night. Naturally, she was terrified. I'd never come up against anything like this, so I advised her to sage the room and pray to God if it happened again. Later that week, at the club, Richard came over to our table, where we were gathered in a group. He sneered, gazing down at my friend, and said, "Did you enjoy the sexy visitor I sent you the other night?" He looked at me and said, "By the way, Janet, you're next on my list!"

I was gobsmacked! My instincts were right about him, and although I was seriously concerned, I didn't show it. Turning to him, I spoke in a very intense but controlled voice and said if he even so much as tried to send me any demon entity, he'd be sorry because I would send it straight back to him. I then stood up to leave, grabbed my friend, and left the club. That night I lit white candles in every room in my house and recited the Lord's Prayer repeatedly. Using the mind power technique, I visualized myself pushing any negative energy away from me and back to him.

The next time we saw Richard at the club, he seemed very disturbed; something was wrong. We watched from afar as security wrestled him to the ground and grabbed a long knife from him. As they dragged him out the door, he looked at Mike and said, "You're next." We later found out he had threatened to stab him.

It is a well-known fact with any magical practice that if you send something evil out and the recipient rejects it, it has nowhere else to go than back to the person who sent it. The entity gains power while traveling around and can terrorize its creator.

The next night, Mike tried to drift off to sleep in his apartment when he sensed movement in the bedroom. A gray, foggy mass of energy grew from the corner of the room, and an unpleasant odor filled the space. As he concentrated on the streetlight peeking through the curtains, the thing expanded to a height of nearly six feet before materializing into a frightening, demon-like entity. He immediately guessed Richard had sent this monster to harm him, as he had been unable to send it to me. Just as I had done, he chanted the Lord's Prayer over and over until the entity slowly disappeared, taking the nauseating smell with it.

A couple of days later, my friend said that Richard had overdosed on pills and whiskey and slashed his wrists in an attempted suicide. We can only assume that his entity found its way back home when we rejected it, and as powerful as he was, he was too naive to cope with the consequences. Richard survived but never regained his sanity. To this day, he is still a resident in a mental health facility.

PROTECTION METHOD 1

IF ANY supernatural entity visits you, dried angelica (Archangelica) is a powerful and pungent herb that repels any demonic invasion. Put a dish of dried angelica in each room of your home, and scatter some on the ground outside the front and rear doors. It is also effective if you wear the herb, so acquire a locket and place some inside or pin a pouch of it to your clothing.

PROTECTION METHOD 2

A CUP of natural sea salt blended with a cup of the dried herb horehound is highly effective at keeping demons away, so sprinkling this on the floor around your bed is the first step for a demon-free night. Having a picture of the Archangel Michael somewhere in the room will also keep them at bay. Before you drift off to sleep, ask Michael to surround you in a positive light and protect you from venturing onto the negative astral planes during sleep.

REVENGE CURSES

THESE CURSES ARE CAST WHEN an individual has been wronged by someone, and are designed to make the other feel regret for their actions. The intention can also be for the other person to experience a similar event and suffer the same emotions that they did. An example would be if a woman went all out to steal a man from another woman, she too would undergo the same fate. These curses are created using three items: a piece of paper, a black pen, and a small black candle. As with any hex, the strength comes from the caster's intention, so during the ritual, they would generate rage and hatred within themselves and focus it entirely on their target. The curser would light the candle and leave it to burn halfway down. Throughout this process, they would very slowly write the name of the person nine times on the piece of paper, all the time keeping their enemy's face in their mind's eye. The paper would be placed next to the candle until it burned out, then ripped into tiny pieces and thrown in the trash.

However, there is always a consequence of any black magic, and in one way or another, the caster will live to regret their actions.

PROTECTION

BLACK TOURMALINE worn alongside lapis lazuli will shield the wearer from any revenge curse. The best way to protect yourself is to wear the crystals as jewelry in a bracelet or necklace. It's essential not to take it off until you are confident the caster has moved on and is not directing ill thoughts toward you.

GENERATIONAL OR ANCESTRAL CURSES

THIS CURSE IS MORE COMMON than we think, and many families bound by the hex probably don't even realize it. The curse may have originated hundreds of years beforehand, or more recently. As with any curse or evil intent toward another, the caster was probably wronged in some way and set out to seek revenge. It could be something as simple as a land dispute hundreds of years ago or even a scorned woman rejected by a married lover. The curse can frequently skip generations or even specific members of the family. It may go dormant for a while before being reactivated by a particular event. Examples of this type of curse can be that infant boys in the family never live above a certain age, or that the family's female members never experience true romantic fulfillment. Any curse is born through the transmission of negative energy, and this is no different. Sometimes, they are activated when a generation turns a certain age. More than one man in the family line can find they suddenly become sterile, might struggle with substance abuse, or never be able to escape poverty.

PROTECTION

GENERATIONAL CURSES are locked into your aura from the moment of your birth, so in this instance, a salt bath or a quick candle ritual won't work.

You can combat this problem and reclaim your power in many ways, but sometimes, breaking every link in the chain is impossible. If you manage to sever your own hex, and other family members still seem affected, they will all need to perform this ritual to escape it once and for all.

This spell calls for it to be cast on the first day of a new moon phase when the energies around you will invite light and change into your life.

Our blood is linked to our ancestors, so you must use a tiny amount of your own blood. You can purchase a finger pricker, the type diabetics use to test their sugar levels, or women can use a small amount of menstrual blood if they prefer.

Write down your mother's maiden name and your father's surname on a piece of paper. If you have a different last name, write yours down as well. Dab each name with a tiny amount of blood. Transfer this paper into a fireproof bowl, take it outside, and place it on a slab or in a safe place. Create a circle of coarse sea salt around the bowl, making sure not to leave any gaps. Set fire to the paper and speak the words below nine times:

"All curses bound to this bloodline, I destroy this day,
I remove these ties from years gone by; I unbind this evil and
send it away."

When you have said the spell nine times, close the ritual by saying the following prayer:

"Angels, I ask thee to send comfort to my ancestors.
Now the curse is lifted; let them rest in peace.
Fill our lives with light from the skies and surround us in your
forever love.
So mote it be."

Collect the ashes from the bowl and flush them down the toilet.

Go inside and remove all your clothing and put it in the washing machine. Take a bath or shower, preferably using some salt for cleansing, and when you are finished, put on fresh, clean clothes. You should now be free of any negative energy attached to your aura, and the curse should be lifted.

PROTECTION FROM CURSES

THERE ARE WAYS WE CAN defend ourselves from this type of psychic attack, regardless of whether we know the person who cursed us or not. Below are some methods that work very well, so choose another if you find one ritual isn't very effective. Often, to make sure our enemies are at bay, we might have to repeat these defensive rituals a few times a month. As with any retaliation to black magic or curses, you must believe your actions will work. Push all the doubts away and trust in your power.

DOORWAY SPELLS

BECAUSE OUR home is our sanctuary and the place we occupy most of the time, often when someone is cursed, the negative energy can linger in the victim's home. Placing protective items at the entrance and exit to a house or dwelling effectively keeps evil of any kind out and can stop a curse from reaching the person. Doorframes are considered quite important as they can act like portals, separating one form of energy from another. Focusing on the doors that separate the outside world from the indoors is the best place to start.

GARLIC AND SALT

WITH A black pen, draw the image of an eye on a single clove of unpeeled garlic and place it in a bag of salt. Fasten the bag and leave it on your front doorstep for three days. The curse will then be lifted and given back to its creator. It is essential to perform this in a neutral frame of mind because if it is done with hatred, you could harm the other person.

RED BRICK DUST

RED BRICK dust, also known as redding, red powder, or red dust, is a magical substance that deflects harmful energy from your home. You can purchase it inexpensively online or make it yourself by shattering a red brick outside with a hammer and grinding it until it resembles fine dust. This age-old method has been employed for many years to lift curses and safeguard a property's occupants. There are two ways to protect the house. The first is to mop the floors throughout the house with a mixture of brick dust and spring water; this is a powerful way to purge the home of any evil. The second method involves sprinkling the dust at the doorways leading in and out, either on the step or the ground.

CRYSTAL DOORFRAMES

CRYSTALS ARE effective at keeping out negativity and can shield the home from evil curses, spirits, and negative people. Before you place the crystals, cleaning the top of the doorframes thoroughly is essential. Smaller crystals are just as active as larger ones, so try to purchase small tumble stones that won't fall off the frame when people open and close the doors.

A combination of jasper, hematite, and tiger's eye creates a confusing energy that most evil intents or curses will fail to penetrate, so situate these on the top of every doorframe in your home.

⚜ ALL-PURPOSE DEFENSE SPELL ⚜

However you've been cursed, sometimes you need to fight fire with fire, and the only way you can safely protect yourself is to mimic how a curse was created in the first place. Most people working on the dark side send curses using a black candle and harmful intentions. If you know who has cursed you, you can concentrate your intent on that particular individual, but if not, you might have to focus solely on removing the curse. In both instances, you will need to make a hex oil, sometimes called "Hell devils" oil. There are many recipes for this online, but the following ingredients make a potent oil that will act as a safety shield.

You will need:
1 teaspoon hot chili seeds (ghost pepper or scotch
  bonnet seeds are best)
1 teaspoon black mustard seeds
1 teaspoon black peppercorns
½ cup pure olive oil

Grind the chili seeds, black mustard seeds, and pep-percorns in a pestle and mortar. While you are doing this, focus your intent on breaking all hexes and curses. When ground together, mix the oil on top of the seeds. Leave to steep overnight.

For the following part, you will need a tall black candle, ensuring it is entirely made of black wax and not dipped. Rub a small amount of the oil onto the wax, massaging the candle for at least five minutes. Say these words three times while you are working the oil into the candle:

"I reject your curse; I don't want your curse; you can have your curse, cast it away.

I refuse your curse; I rebuff your curse; I stamp on your curse, cast it away.

I discard your curse; I return your curse; it is your curse, not mine; cast it away."

Place the candle in a suitable holder and light it. Next, repeat the chant above three times; only this time, you need to stamp your feet and virtually shout the spell. Put as much vigor into it as possible and believe in your magi-cal ability. You will need a lot of energy to return this curse to its sender, so don't hold back.

TAKE A SALT BATH

GOOD USUALLY trumps evil, so when black magic is present, the only successful way to counteract the curse is to balance everything with a positive magic spell.

Run a bath and add a cup of sea salt, a tablespoon of baking soda, and a few drops of tea tree oil. These three ingredients will decontaminate anything untoward, allowing only positive energy to surround you. While the tub is filling with water, take a wooden spoon and stir in a clockwise motion. Recite this incantation at least three or four times until you can step into the water:

"Purified water, shield me from harm, create a vibration of peace and calm.
Bathe my body, bathe my soul; protection from curses is my goal."

After completing this incantation, close the spell by saying, "So mote it be."

Once submerged in the water, close your eyes, visualize the salt and oils eliminating any dark energy around you, and focus on the water protecting every part of your body. After about ten minutes of this meditation, stand up and wash your body thoroughly using some foamy soap. Next, shampoo your hair twice and rinse with fresh water. You need to remain in the tub for at least thirty minutes; this should banish any negative energy you might have around you. This ritual will not work in the shower, so if you don't have a bathtub, ask a friend who has one if you can use it.

TOURMALINE WAND

TOURMALINE IS renowned for its protective properties against black magic, and for the ultimate defense, using a larger tourmaline wand seems to be more successful than a smaller type. Before you begin, cleanse the crystal of any energy it might have picked up in transit by lighting a sage incense stick and running it through the smoke (see page 180). Another way to rid crystals of any previous vibes is to leave them outside overnight on a dry night of a full moon phase; this not only cleanses them but also empowers them.

For this ritual, you will need to ask someone to help you. Give them the crystal, then stand with your legs slightly apart and your arms outstretched to the side. Your helper must hold the pointed end of the crystal at the top of your head and sweep it from the center of your head to the right-hand side three or four times. Imagine the crystal catching the curse and dragging it away from you. Next, starting at the center of your head again, they must repeat the sweeping action, this time to the left-hand side. Move down to the neck area and repeat the steps above the chest, arms, and stomach. This procedure must be carried out on every part of your body, moving from the center to the right and left, traveling down throughout the body until they reach your feet.

When the sweeping is complete, keep the crystal in your vicinity for at least a month. It will act as a talisman of sorts, drawing any unwanted energy away from you like a magnet. If you are relaxing at home, keep it in the same room, take it to bed at night, place it on your nightstand, and keep it in your purse or pocket when you are out and about. If you still feel vulnerable, repeat the sweeping ritual again.

※ A POWERFUL CANDLE SPELL ※

You will need to source black and white spell candles. These candles are approximately ten centimeters tall and can be purchased easily online using the keywords "spell candles." For this ritual, the candle colors are significant; the black represents the curse, and the white signifies a remedy.

Begin with the white candle, and with a sharp knife or pin, scratch your full name and the following words into the wax—"protection from curse."

Next, on the black candle, inscribe your name again and these words—"return the curse to its sender." If you know who has put a curse on you, scratch their full name into the wax as well.

You have to create a spell-breaking oil to anoint your candle. Try to purchase high-quality essential oils for this part. Please note this oil will work in breaking any spell.

You will need:
A small bowl to blend the oil
5 milliliters base oil or vegetable oil
4 drops tea tree oil
4 drops basil oil
2 drops lavender oil
pinch of garlic salt

All the ingredients above possess powerful curse-breaking properties, so to begin, you need to blend all the oils in a bowl before finally adding the garlic salt. Leave the bowl overnight to work its magic. The next day, dip your finger in the oil and, starting at the top of each inscribed candle, run your finger in a downward line until it reaches the bottom. Put the candles in holders and place them in the center of any table or work surface, black to the left and white to the right. The table will act as your altar.

> *More items you will need:*
> 1 cup coarse sea salt
> dragon's blood incense stick
> picture of Archangel Michael
> some meditation music
> small bell (any kind)
> piece of clear quartz crystal (any size)

Create a circle of salt on the floor in front of the table, large enough for you to stand inside. Light a dragon's blood incense stick and situate this behind the candles.

You aim is to invite Archangel Michael, the highest-ranking angel of protection, to help you lift the curse. You can download and print out a picture of him online and rest this somewhere on the table. If you can't access a printer, find an image online, put his picture on your cell phone, and place this on the table instead.

To begin the ritual, you must ensure the house is quiet. No children or pets running around. It might be best to conduct it when everyone is out, and you have the place to yourself.

Play some meditation music on a low volume, creating the right ambience for your spell, then light the candles.

Take a small bell and ring it over the table for around

thirty seconds to clear the workspace of any negative energies.

Stand inside the circle of salt and hold the crystal in your right hand. Point it to the table and say the following incantation twelve times:

"I call forth Archangel Michael to aid me in my plight.
Shield me with your wings, cloak me in your light.
Angels of the universe, I call upon your power this day,
Remove this hex that plagues me; drive the curse away."

When you have spoken the spell twelve times, bow your head and say, "And so it is."

You may notice that any negative energy in the room will lift, as when Archangel Michael is summoned, he often leaves behind an angelic presence. It's important not to blow out the candles; leave them to burn down with the incense. Keep the crystal in your living room for a week or so, as it will continue to dispel lingering energies. You will know the prayer has worked because you will feel differently and have a more positive mental attitude.

We know there are a lot of steps to this ritual, but it really works.

GHOSTS OR ALIENS?

SINCE THE BEGINNING OF TIME, there has always been considerable interest in demons, monsters, and otherworldly beings, but we have to ask, are they not the same thing? Indigenous people have made drawings in caves of alien-type beings; some even appear to be wearing space suits and helmets. There is a theory that aliens have been around from the beginning to aid and help humanity progress to a more sophisticated level, improve our consciousness, and advance our technology. Nowadays, there is global fear that they will wipe us out by germ warfare or, worse, invade us en masse. Others believe we are polluting our planet to such an extent that soon they will have no choice but to reveal themselves to us and try to help us eradicate our problem with global warming. Conspiracy theorists suggest the governments of the world have been hiding their existence for decades for fear of global panic. Still, since nearly all of us carry a camera around with us daily on our smartphones, we are increasingly reporting these sightings and uploading the content to the internet.

Many believe that governments will run out of excuses and have no choice but to inform us of their presence. Some even contend that news broadcasts and shows like *Ancient Aliens* and other paranormal TV series are slowly drip-feeding us information in preparation for their arrival.

The thought of being attacked by these unknown creatures is the stuff of nightmares, especially when so many people believe they have been abducted and taken into crafts. Abductees liken their experiences to psychic attacks as they report that aliens use mind control to communicate with us.

Because ghosts and spirits can sometimes resemble glowing orbs or lights, some believers in extraterrestrial life have hypothesized that these reported sightings could be, in fact, extraterrestrial.

Some Native Americans compelled to march during the Trail of Tears in the early 1830s claimed to have seen an odd ball of light floating close to the border between Oklahoma and Missouri. The light, around the size of a basketball, was named "spook light" for centuries. The ancients believed it to be the spirit of two Native American lovers searching for each other at night, or even the devil holding a lantern.

Tourists visit the area where the spook light appears, especially around Halloween. According to scientists, it could be a natural gas leak or traffic lights reflecting off a nearby river. However, this doesn't account for sightings many years before modern vehicles were invented. For centuries people have described orbs or balls of light in the distance that resemble some type of alien craft when viewed up close.

Most of the time, ghosts are invisible to the human eye, and if they do show themselves, they can often be seen as wisps of light, similar to funnel ghosts. Perhaps the aliens have developed a technology that reflects light to maintain invisibility, which allows them to keep a close eye on the human race without us even knowing; this could explain why so many unidentified anomalies are reported around war zones or nuclear facilities. We all know the planet is environmentally unstable, and who is to say that if we continue to contaminate our Earth with pollution, this won't also impact other planets in our galaxy? It makes sense if aliens, who are thousands, if not millions, of years ahead of us as far as technology is concerned, avoid being seen by using a cloaking device to observe us.

Nearly half of Americans and millions of other individuals across the globe believe that we are not alone in the universe. Countless people have reported being abducted by aliens, and some have even had implants removed from their bodies, which scientists later stated are not made from materials found on this Earth. Abductees report being taken onto a ship and restrained on a stainless-steel-like table, surrounded by small creatures, commonly known as the grays, who ultimately control them. The victims find their bodies are paralyzed, and rather than speaking directly to them, the aliens communicate through telepathy. Some abductees report that their transmissions are revealed through apocalyptic images, showing storms so intense that the sidewalks are lifted from the ground, and uncontrollable fires and floods engulf the planet. What is harrowing is that the aliens lack empathy when performing these experiments, showing no mercy or respect to the humans. When the victim is returned to Earth, they might lose hours of time or find themselves in a completely different location, together with strange marks on their body where they were medically interfered with.

CASE STUDY: ELVA HYBRIDS

Over the years myself, my husband, daughter, and grandchildren have all encountered something we believe to be alien. From an early age, I sensed that aliens were on our planet, and now, in my seventies, I still deem it to be true.

My first encounter was when I was four, and I was drifting out of sleep. I saw a vast room with huge ceiling-to-floor glass tubes filled with liquid. Inside these large vessels were a variety of naked human beings in a comatose state. An electrical-created voice said to me, "These are hybrids." When I woke, I relayed my experience to my mother and asked her what a hybrid was. She brushed me off and told me I had far too much imagination.

As an adult, I continued to have strange experiences. One morning at 5 A.M., I woke up when suddenly I felt an electrical presence in the room. My heart started pounding, and I instinctively knew I would be taken. The alien mind control was so powerful I was utterly paralyzed. I saw some small gray creatures around my bed, with huge, black wraparound eyes, staring intently into my face. They showed no empathy; I felt like a lab rat waiting for inspection. For a moment, I found my voice and started to scream, and then instantly, a mask was placed over my mouth and I fell unconscious. At around 7 A.M., I awoke, and the memory of what happened was clear in my mind. I thought it must have been a dream for a moment, but I looked down at the inside of my arm and saw what looked like a cigarette burn on it. There were eight tiny needle pricks around the outer circle of the burn and one significant piercing black mark in the middle. I took a photo of the mark and still look at it today.

CASE STUDY: IAN

My whole life, I was skeptical about claims of aliens and abductions until something strange happened. One night, I went to bed as usual and had a weird dream. I was taken to a strange spaceship and examined by small, childlike creatures with just four long fingers on each of their hands. Their bodies were slender and gray, with huge black, glassy eyes. I woke in the early hours of the morning in a cold sweat and put it down to being a nightmare of sorts. Suddenly, I felt very disoriented. My bedroom had an en suite shower and a red telltale light inside the door. I couldn't see this light from my usual sleeping position because a cupboard would block the view. In a sleepy state, I looked directly at the light and reached for the bedside table to turn on the lamp, but it wasn't there. Hastily, I got out of bed to turn on the main overhead light, and when I turned around, nothing was as it should have been. The whole bed had somehow been rotated 180 degrees, with the headboard and pillows where the foot of the bed should be. I stood there in stunned silence.

The following day, I kept seeing flashbacks of the strange dream, but the harder I tried to focus on what had happened, the quicker the images disappeared. It was as if some weird force was overriding my memories, and I could no longer control my thoughts or feelings. I also noticed two vivid marks, like needle pricks, on the inside of my wrist, which were right over my vein. They had not been there the day before. Today, twenty years later, those marks remain. My only explanation of this weird event is that I was abducted, brought back in haste, and the aliens had not paid attention to details.

CASE STUDY: CAROLINE

I'm a healer and counselor in the county of Devon, England, and aliens have repeatedly abducted me from the age of twelve. My first memory was experienced on a school trip as I looked out the bus window. I caught sight of a silver craft with bright lights hovering over a lane. Furtively, I glanced around the bus to see if anyone else had seen it, but nobody had. My next recollection was one New Year's Eve at the family home; I was lying in bed and saw a bright light outside the window. I had a strange experience where my body froze, and then I *lost all sense of time and fell asleep. Some months later, I decided to go on a healing course with four other therapists. In one of the sessions, I was asked to meditate, and as I drifted off, I began to have a vivid recollection of an earlier encounter. I saw myself in a silver spaceship, shackled to a cold metal operating table. I looked around and spotted numerous other individuals in similar circumstances, all appearing to be investigated medically by aliens. Suddenly, I was surrounded by four alien grays. They were short and spindly, with no mouth or nose, and as I looked into the large black eyes, I was overpowered with an unusual feeling of familiarity. They seemed to be communicating telepathically, first with me and then with one another, so in my mind, I asked them what they were doing. The grays replied that they knew little about human emotions and were interested in my rare sensitivity.*

I told them that if they were to keep experimenting on me, the least they could do would be to give me a healthy womb, as I had tried for fourteen years to have children with no success. At first, the request was denied, but one of the more senior grays finally agreed. They indicated that it was a trade-off, and if I worked with people on an emotional level, I would assist them in understanding humans better so that they might help them in the future. A painless surgical procedure was then performed, and as I drifted in and out of consciousness, I was shown the faces of three children; all were blond, although the middle child looked fragile. When I asked why the child was delicate, they did not reply but reassured me that they would continue to protect me and the children from all harm. One month after the meditation, I became pregnant; in time, all three of my children were born. My son (the middle child) was born with cystic fibrosis but is healthy and active against all odds. Even though it was an ordeal, I am eternally grateful the aliens blessed me with three beautiful children.

CASE STUDY: ANNA

I'm an author, teacher, and university lecturer who lives in the South of England.

When I was still living in my home country of Zimbabwe, about fifteen years ago, I had a most incredible, otherworldly experience in the form of a vivid dream.

A couple of days before the dream, my mother and I had returned home from a weekend at my sister's farm, about two hours' drive from Harare, and we were shocked to find that our house had been ransacked. As with many properties in Harare, we had burglar bars on every window, security gates across the doors, a fenced garden, and a locked gate; this hadn't deterred the burglars, who'd sawn through the lock on the gate, entering the property and managing to force their way into the house by removing tiles off the roof and cutting through the ceiling. Their entry point was through the ceiling in my bedroom. The house was trashed, especially my room, which had fallen debris scattered from the ceiling. My clothes, books, papers, and belongings were chaotically strewn everywhere. The overwhelming feeling of violation left my mother and me speechless as we tried to slowly collect things together and tidy up the wreckage, gradually realizing what had been taken.

While we waited a few days for the ceiling in my room to be repaired, I slept on a camp bed in my mother's bedroom; it was a comfort to stay close as we were both shaken and felt unprotected by what had happened.

It must've been about two days later that I had the dream, what I call my "visitation." I was standing alone in a space that seemed to be in a shaded area, and looking ahead saw what seemed like a sizeable silver spacecraft landing in front of me. I clearly remember a sort of door opening and a very bright light emanating from inside the spaceship as a ramp was lowered and people began to come out. Then I saw a very tall man standing in front of me. He had a slightly Asian appearance with black hair that was almost shoulder length. I felt I could trust him as he held out his hand to greet me. I responded to him, and we shook hands, and as we did so, he pressed my hand at the base of my thumb with his thumb; I remember feeling that pressure very clearly and was reassured by it.

We were then in the lounge at my house. He had arrived with a group of men dressed identically in blue and black satin robes with a type of headdress. The tall man himself was also in a robe, but it was more opulent, and he seemed to be the one in charge and was the only person who spoke to me.

As I was standing in the lounge with the leader, I asked him: "Do you know what has happened in this house recently?"

He answered: "Yes, that is why we're here; we came to protect you from this evil."

The men who had accompanied him worked in groups of two or three. They went down the corridor and into the rooms of the house. What fascinated me was that they were carrying small golden ornamental branches with them, to which they were attaching golden leaves that they had crafted. The result was that each room in the house was decorated with these beautiful, bright golden trees about a meter or so high.

Suddenly I found myself awake, and as I opened my eyes, I saw stunning flashes of colored light reflecting off the crystals hanging in the window. It was bouncing off the walls as they spun in the morning breeze. I felt happy and remarkably blessed and quietly said, "Thank you for my protection." Although I was not quite sure who I was thanking, I knew I had experienced something extraordinary. All the bad vibes had somehow been removed from my house. It was cleansed, refreshed, and safe once more.

KUNDALINI

IN HINDUISM, THE KUNDALINI IS seen as a feminine divine force at the base of the spine, often cited as the "sleeping serpent." By stimulating this force, it is believed that an individual's divine essence can be awakened, especially if the person has been going through psychic attacks, violence, and hard times. Their essence will be cleansed and recharged.

The kundalini, be it rising or awakened, can be harrowing and sometimes called the "little death." Many describe it as a unique experience, like a spiritual reboot or awakening. Because of the inability to move when this happens, some people are fearful and think they are under psychic attack. The experience feels like an electric charge emanating from the base of the spine and then moving up through the various chakra points in the body before emerging from the crown chakra at the head. Commonly, the kundalini will usually happen at night, while in bed, and can come on quite unexpectedly. The sleeper will awaken to a strange tingling sensation throughout the body, which then develops into a deeper, more profound experience.

Some have said that if they were feeling very low, unwell, or challenged by life, the cleansing and uplifting experience of the kundalini raised their spirits and renewed their energy to move forward. Often it will trigger more significant insights into their situation, and sudden resolutions to the problems surrounding them will appear.

No one knows if this is a spiritual or otherworldly occurrence, but whatever it is, it's not a regular event. The amount of time it happens to an individual varies from person to person. Some might have it five or six times a year, others just once in a lifetime.

Those interested in alien theories believe that when the kundalini is in action, the extraterrestrial beings might be adjusting the person's DNA or uploading or downloading information from the person's mind.

The awakened kundalini can be self-triggered by meditation, chanting, or other methods such as yoga and transcendental meditation, but more often than not, it happens naturally.

BINAURAL BEATS

BINAURAL BEATS ARE ALSO THOUGHT to help a person experience the rising kundalini and work with meditational music to soothe the soul and bring delta activity to the brain waves, lengthening stage three of dream sleep. It works only with headphones and a frequency of three hertz, which will enhance all areas of the brain in around fifteen minutes. For safety, it is suggested not to overdose on this powerful music because it might cause depression. If listened to for ten minutes in the morning, many have said it boosts a person's energy for the rest of the day.

YouTube has a variety of this music available to listen to. The benefits bring strength to the soul to ward off psychic attacks and are purported to be a quicker way to enter deep meditation.

CASE STUDY: LEANNA
EXPLODING HEAD SYNDROME

The French philosopher Adrien Baillet first reported EHS (exploding head syndrome) in the seventeenth century. This frightening condition is believed to affect 10 percent of the world's population, and although scientists know little about it, they suppose it's a form of sleep paralysis. Those like me who are unfortunate enough to suffer with it hear loud bangs, like explosions, gunshot sounds, or cymbals crashing inside the head while the body is just drifting off to sleep. Often when a sufferer is in a deep sleep, they can be woken up by a loud sound that can be felt in every nerve in the body.

I had my first experience of EHS when I was around six years of age, and I remember a tinnitus sound starting very softly in my ears and then gradually getting louder and louder until I felt as if I couldn't bear it for another second. In the end, the noise of cymbals crashing filled my head. The term "exploding head syndrome" is apt because it feels like the head is about to blow up. Initially, this would happen to me around once a month; there were no triggers or warnings, it would simply occur out of the blue. As I got older, the symptoms changed somewhat, and often, it would begin with me hearing people whisper in my ears, although I could never make out what they were saying. The whispering, like with the tinnitus sound, grew louder and louder until I heard a single gunshot. Throughout the experience, I couldn't move a muscle. I couldn't speak or move any part of my body until the ordeal was over, sometimes up to ten minutes at a time. Mother took me to the doctor on more than one occasion, but the condition was unheard of, and no one knew how to treat it.

As I approached my forties, EHS would occur more frequently, often happening every night. Normally, I would fight the noises, but one night, back in 2015, I decided not to struggle against it. Instead, I relaxed into the experience to see what would happen. As the tinnitus sound increased, I fought the urge to retaliate until it reached a crescendo. As the noise dissipated, I had what I thought was a hallucination. My eyes were closed, but I saw a black TV screen with a clear image of Donald Trump standing outside the White House. If that wasn't weird enough, a gray alien was on each side of him.

The vision vanished as quickly as it came, and I sat up feeling bewildered. The next night, my parents were over for supper, and as we were enjoying our meal, I told them what had happened the night before. Mother was intrigued, but Dad chuckled and said, "I can't ever see Donald Trump being president, Leanna," and told me I was probably dreaming. I agreed with him, as even though it was common knowledge that Trump had toyed with the idea of the presidency, we all thought it was extremely unlikely that he would be voted in.

Once I realized this exploding head couldn't kill me, during every experience, I continued to refrain from fighting against it, and so the hallucinations kept coming. On one occasion, my black TV screen showed me an ancient leather-bound journal. With each turn of the page, I saw a photograph of a baby. There were around thirty pictures, and some were very old, perhaps depicting a time before the camera was even invented. I recognized each baby immediately until the final pages showed the photos of my two boys in this life when they were around eighteen months old.

The strangest was when my adult son, who had a small cabin at the edge of our property, began telling us that he was seeing aliens in the night. He told us they would enter his room and paralyze him so he couldn't move. These visits happened every night, so he relayed a different story each morning. My son has a form of autism, and so he thinks very differently from us a lot of the time. He is highly intelligent and entirely grounded, so when he started relaying these tales, I really took notice of him. One morning he came in and said he hadn't slept at all and that the aliens had taken him to another galaxy through a wormhole before showing him another planet. He said the planet was beautiful, with vibrant surface foliage, lakes, rivers, and oceans. They then took him "inside" the planet where the occupants lived. He asked them why they didn't live on the surface, and they replied that they were preserving their world and not contaminating it. When they returned him to his bed, he remembers them placing him the wrong way around so that his head was at the base of the bed and his feet at the top. When he awoke, he was facing the wrong way; this seems common with those who believe they've been abducted. I was concerned and didn't know what to think, so I told him when they visited again, he was to tell the aliens that I would like to speak with them. I said it didn't matter what time of day or night they wanted to come; I would be happy to see them. That night, I purposely left the back door unlocked so they would have easy access to my property if they chose to take me up on my offer. I drifted off to sleep at about 11 P.M. until I awoke with an exploding head experience at precisely 1:45 A.M., but unlike before, I wasn't paralyzed, and I could open my eyes. I saw hundreds of illuminated lights moving around the bedroom in the darkness. I looked over to my left and saw my husband sleeping soundly beside me, so I remained awake and sat and waited for the rest of the night, trying to get a connection to whoever was creating them. As the sun came up, the lights disappeared.

My son approached the house the following day and said, "Well? Did they come to see you?" I replied, "I think so." He said he'd relayed my message and watched them walk through the back door and into the house. I asked him what time he spoke to them to ensure neither of us was delusional. He replied, "At 1:45 A.M."

Another incident happened just recently. Like many others worldwide, I suffer from osteoarthritis in my left hip, and when the weather is wet or cold, the pain gets so bad I can barely put my foot on the floor. I was experiencing a lot of pain, which had been hounding me for a week or more. As I lay in my bed, I closed my eyes and asked the angels if they could possibly give me some healing. As I was drifting off to sleep, I was awoken by a sharp fizzing pain on the left side of my waist, and when I quickly opened my eyes, there was an alien face inches away from mine. It seemed shocked that I had woken up, and as it hastily retreated, I saw a long syringe-like object in its hand. Then the alien vanished. The next day, I was pain-free and continued to be for at least four months.

I have since surrendered to my exploding head experiences and now try very hard to "go with it." Each time it happens to me, I undergo some form of hallucination, and oddly, they show future events that later come to pass. Nowadays, professionals describe exploding head syndrome as a form of sleep paralysis, where the different parts of the brain fail to shut down properly before sleeping. Still, if that were the case, surely, I wouldn't be predicting the future with my visions? We will probably never know whether it is a prophecy or an extraterrestrial visitation, but for now, I am just happy to see where they lead.

Part IV

NATURE'S PROTECTION

HERBS, TREES, AND PLANT LIFE have been used from the beginning of time for rituals, nutrition, medicine, and protection. One of our dear friends now passed over once remarked that for every ailment, disease, or symptom, there is a plant, herb, or tree created by nature to heal and, most important, offer other forms of spiritual protection to human beings and animals. Of course, every culture worldwide has superstitions about plants; often, these are tales passed down through the generations. We humans take the flowers and shrubs that grow in our natural surroundings for granted and are unaware of their power and effect, some of which may even be able to protect us from unseen, harmful occurrences. Some people might mock these old wives' tales saying that they are nothing more than fanciful ideas, but we should pay attention to what our ancestors believed, for there might actually be some truth to it.

All of the below-listed herbs and plants are thought to possess the ability to protect against psychic attack and shield a person from spiritual intrusion in one way or another. Online stores offer most of the varieties at reasonable prices.

ANGELICA

Archangelica

In folklore, this prime protector was used to summon the angels to protect homes and families. It was also used in banishment rituals to free a place of evil spirits, especially those whose negative energies would be difficult to assuage.

To cleanse the house of evil, sprinkle a handful of angelica in each corner of every room. It will form a protective barrier and dispel negative energies.

To ward off black magic, fill a small drawstring pouch with dried angelica and pin it to your clothing. Placing the bag under a pillow at night is said to have the powerful effect of shielding the wearer from night demons. The angelica root can also be ground into powder, and can be used as aromatic incense.

ASPHODEL

Asphodeline

A white star-shaped lily, asphodel dates back to ancient Greece and was popular in Victorian society. The flower represented peace after death and commemorated the loss of a loved one. It could also remind the mourner of bitterness, regret, and unfinished business with the beloved, which should have been rectified before their passing.

If the departed soul was unhappy, it could haunt its

family, which could detain its entrance to the spirit realm. Holding the flower in a place of stillness is said to bring the departed person to their side one last time for a loving connection and perhaps to resolve the sad times between them.

Because this plant is suitable for clearing spirits from properties, mediums sent in to clear houses often hold a bowl of asphodel petals while they are helping to cross over a ghost.

BASIL

Basilius

Holy basil, *Ocimum tenuiflorum,* is the most effective plant for defending against demons and hostile ghosts. If you have trouble acquiring this, you can use any other variety. Making a spiritual Teflon spray is as simple as mixing a cup of holy water with ten basil leaves. Transfer the water into a plastic bottle and spray it all around the floors of the home. Any spirits or residual energy will be cast out.

BETONY

Stachys officinalis

Betony is purported to be a protective and cleansing herb. In folklore, it was believed that if the plant was eaten or a sprig of it pinned to clothing, it protected the wearer's body and soul from dark forces and placed an invisible barrier to ward against powerful psychic attacks.

Growing this herb in pots around the house will prevent evil spirits from entering. You can also push a few sprigs into your pillowcase to avoid astral attacks or nightmares.

BIRCH

Betonica officinalis

The birch tree is celebrated at the festival of Samhain, which is the start of the Celtic year. It is also a favorite wood for a witch's broom. Medieval folk would hang a branch of this sacred tree over doorways to ward off the evil eye and mischievous demons. When felons were beaten as punishment, the birch twigs were used to hopefully drive out the fiends and cleanse a person's soul.

If you have a large enough garden, planting this tree will keep demons away; if not, search the local area and keep some birch twigs in a tall pot beside the entrance to a home.

CELANDINE

Ficaraia verna

This beautiful bright yellow plant helps remove negative energies and brings courage to weaker individuals. It's usually best to plant it in a large pot outside, as it's hardy and will spread rapidly. Although celandine is used in medicine, we advise against ingesting it raw, as it is highly toxic. In ancient folklore, it could break curses or the evil eye, thus freeing a person from entrapment.

If you believe you are cursed or think someone might have sent you the evil eye, grow celandine in the garden, as it will act as a positive defense.

CLOVE

Syzygium aromaticum

Grown in Molucca in Indonesia, the immature red flower buds are plucked from the tree and resemble rusty nails. They are used in medicine, and were highly prized and worth a fortune in times gone by. Cloves are purported to protect a person from psychic attacks or premeditated black magic. They have a fiery energy that boosts spell-crafting or enhances powerful protection from the evil eye. When cloves are burnt, they are an equal replacement for white sage.

If a ghost is haunting a house where a young child or baby resides and you are worried they are communicating with the youngster, place a bowl of cloves in a dish up high, perhaps on the top of a wardrobe. Spirits don't like them and will steer clear.

DANDELION

Taraxacum

To gardeners, this is an irritating weed that blooms in the spring. Its bright yellow flowers can be made into wine and eaten in salads. They have numerous health-giving properties and vitamins. If a person is trying to cope with psychic attacks or negative people, this plant offers rebirth and a return to a better life. European witches believe the dandelion can grant special wishes and protect people from unseen forces.

If your dreams are disturbing or you have unsavory nighttime visitors, place a handful of dandelion petals and some of the clean roots in a bath of water and bathe in them before bed. The purifying energies of the plant will permeate your aura and protect you from any evil entity.

DILL

Anethum graveolens

This herb has a variety of magical uses. In the past, it was thought to guard against black magic and witchcraft, so it was placed inside bundles or talismans and carried by those who needed protection. However, it was also believed to be a lucky plant that promised prosperity and good fortune. In Europe, brides would place a sprig in their bouquet to bring peace and happiness to the marriage.

If you want to ensure your home is protected, tie a bunch of fresh dill with some string and hang it above the doors at the entrance to your home. This will stop any evil spirits or unpleasant entities from entering.

DRAGON'S BLOOD

Dracaena draco

Dragon's blood is a subtropical tree native to the Canary Islands and is found in many parts of the Middle East,

Indonesia, China, Central America, and numerous other countries. Since pagan times the red sap extracted from the resin of the tree has been used for medicine, incense, magic, rites, and protection against all things sinister. It's also used for varnish and perfume. As it has a powerful, heady aroma and is linked to many spiritual practices; it is revered and valued highly. It also has powerful banishing properties to rid people and places of demons. According to many witches and spiritualists, smudging with dragon's blood is preferable to using sage bundles to rid homes of evil spirits. Additionally, it helps deepen meditation, aids in soul work, and purifies ceremonial activities to achieve a more serene equilibrium.

If any form of ghost, demon, or poltergeist haunts your house, burn sage and dragon's blood smudging sticks simultaneously and wave the smoke all over the house. While doing this, say the following chant out loud three times in each room:

"You are not welcome here. You will not stay; I cast you away."

ELDER

Sambucus nigra

In today's world, we are more accustomed to drinking elderflower wine and elderflower cordial. However, the arboreal power of this tree has a deep history steeped in magic, rites, and protection. In ancient times, the elder was revered across Northern Europe as people believed that potent spirits resided in trees to ward off the devil and witches. Also, the dried elder leaves were hung around the necks of family members, especially the men, to enhance prosperity and good crop yield.

If you want to keep sinister spirits away, make a small wooden cross about ten centimeters high from some of the smaller branches, and then bind them together with a red cord or ribbon to add to its power. Leave it on view in the home, and it should keep negative spirits at bay.

ELM

Ulmus procera

In Celtic mythology, the tall, noble elm was linked with the underworld and had a strong affinity with elves and nature spirits that were said to guard the burial mounds of family graves and the associated passage into the underworld. The elm's history has always been linked to death, much like the yew. In ancient folklore, dreaming of the elm tree could predict death or give the dreamer information for their future protection.

If you want to try to communicate with any ghost or spirit in your home, take a handful of elm leaves and dry them for a few weeks. When they are wilting, hold them while you meditate and ask the ghost to show itself to you. If this is done correctly, you might witness a ghostly apparition during the coming days. However, this is only for the brave, and if you think you have a hostile spirit or demon, don't try it.

FUMARIA

Muralist

The fumitory plant has long been revered as having mystical powers and was mainly used in witchcraft for love spells and affairs of the heart. Fumaria's resin is made into incense, and the smoke is said to purify areas. This powerful uncrossing herb cleanses, performs well in exorcisms, and reverses hexes. It can expel disruptive spirits from the home and rid a person of possession. Many folks are unaware a sinister being possesses them, but fumaria is said to sense this and help root out and dispatch the demon.

You can purchase fumaria tea inexpensively online, so if you think someone is possessed, make the sufferer drink a cup of this tea daily.

FERN

Tracheophyte

Often called living lace. These plants are said to have been around for 400 million years; therefore, their meanings and traditions are buried deep within our psyche. Indigenous people would use them for protection against spiritual enemies or invading tribes. The oil from some fern species was used to treat mental illnesses, or those experiencing demonic possession. Its uplifting benefits are cleansing from all that is negative, allowing new beginnings and happiness.

Growing one in your garden is said to help rid the area of hostile spirits and bring good luck and upliftment of the soul.

GARLIC

Allium sativum

This pungent herb originated in Middle Asia and is in most people's cupboards. It not only provides us with a wealth of health benefits, garlic is also a well-known protector against many supernatural creatures like vampires and zombies. In medieval times the bulbs were strung together and nailed over the doorways and windows of the homeowner. The family would consume as much as possible as a cure-all for protection against evil spirits.

Witches use this ingredient in many of their spells and will sleep with a couple of cloves on their bedside table. It is also said to amplify the powers of other herbs.

To keep out evil spirits, peel a clove of garlic and rub it around all the doorframes in the home.

GARLIC (WILD)

Allium ursinum

Wild garlic grows in woodland areas and spreads like mad. Every part of the plant can be eaten from the stem to the delicate white flowers, leaves, and bulbs. It also deters slugs. Magically, it offers the same protections as traditional garlic; if it grows naturally in the garden, it will protect the home and land from psychic attack.

CASE STUDY: BELETA
NATURE KNOWS BEST

Many years ago, my neighbors discovered I was a clairvoyant and began harassing me. They were devoutly religious and thought I was in league with the devil, so they would shun me at any opportunity. I was worried that they might inadvertently cast me with the evil eye, so I spent much time ensuring I put protection in place. After one particularly unpleasant incident with the neighbors, suddenly, wild garlic started to grow on either side of the driveway to my bungalow. As we live on a sprawling estate, I wondered how it had gotten there and could only assume it was bird given. It spread very quickly but in a controlled way and really did look pretty. Many people remarked about it, and I let friends dig up clumps to take home for the table. I now believe the garlic is a sign that I have spiritual protection, and since then, thankfully, the neighbors have become less aggressive.

GINKGO

Biloba

This tree is believed to have outlived the dinosaurs and has existed for 350 million years, and is also known as the "living fossil." Japanese people and Buddhist monks grew it around their temples and pagodas to protect against the atmospheric fire demons. The leaves are an attractive shade of green and, in the autumn, change to a dazzling yellow. It has numerous health benefits and is claimed to bring luck and protection.

Because of this tree's significant amount of magical energy, if you have been through any supernatural ordeal, the ginkgo can help heal the mind and soul. Take a small branch or piece of bark and carry it around with you for as long as possible to be calm again.

HIGH JOHN THE CONQUEROR

Ipomoea jalapa

It has a pink trumpet flower head and trailing leaves, and the root is said to be magical. This plant initially grew wild in eastern America, and is very popular in hoodoo magic. Its name comes from John the Conqueror, an African prince sold into slavery.

To destroy hostile magic, evil spells, and hexes and protect against financial ruin, especially when others are out to destroy a person's character, dry some of the roots and carry them in a mojo bag or pouch. It will act as a powerful, protective amulet.

HOLLY

Llex verticillate

Holly is considered a masculine plant, so its magical protective properties are said to work better if carried by men. That doesn't mean it won't work for women. According to legend, bringing the leaves inside during the winter would protect fairies from the cold and ensure they were good to humans residing in the home.

To safeguard yourself from curses, make a wand from a holly branch and whittle the end of the stick to a point. Ask someone to draw a circle around you, pointing the tip at the ground. You can also burn the leaves to break a hex and protect the house from evil spirits.

HOREHOUND (ALSO KNOWN AS SOLDIER'S TEA)

Ballota

This herb is related to the mint family and is traditionally known as a healing plant. It has a distinct odor and is used for coughs, colds, and as an expectorant. The white tubular blossoms are edible, and the leaves are green and furry. It has the benefits of keeping the mind strong and focused, creating mental clarity, and balancing erratic energies. When an exorcism occurs, the seeds are scattered in the four corners of a room, and the victim will have a circle of the seeds surrounding them. Wearing an amulet of horehound protects the wearer against black magic and sorcery.

IVY

Hedera helix

In days gone by, ivy was given to a bride and groom for everlasting love and devotion. In Celtic culture, it represented the soul aspiring to gain life experiences through meditation and introspection. In Scotland, ivy was encouraged to grow near cattle to protect them from mischievous elementals and ensure the cow's milk was not stolen.

Nowadays, to have some ivy in the garden is said to ward off spooks, the evil eye, and malevolent spirits. People in the UK are superstitious about cutting down large amounts of ivy and if this is done, they will move house.

INULA MAGNIFICA

Giant Fleabane

Inula, also known as giant fleabane, is quite mysterious, and only a little information about it has ever been recorded. On Midsummer's Eve or solstice, our ancestors would gather the large yellow daisies from the meadows and make bouquets and garlands from them, mixing them with other magical blooms for protection against evil spirits, sprites, and fairies.

The leaves of this plant are thought to be powerful enough to banish an evil spirit. If your house is haunted, bring a few handfuls of inula flowerheads into the kitchen, and submerge them in a bowl of bottled spring water for a day. The following morning, drain the water, transfer it into a bottle, and spray it all around the home. The water will act as a carrier, and any hostile ghosts or entities will leave.

JUNIPER

Juniperus

Juniper is a coniferous bush bearing purple berries found in Asia, Europe, Africa, and America. It has medicinal properties and is used as an aid for digestive issues. In ancient times its aromatic wood was burned to cleanse temples from any buildup of negative energies and was said to gift a person with psychic awareness. This sacred shrub is said to grant protection and was used in funeral rites and exorcisms in the past.

To eliminate any demonic energy in your home, purchase about fifty grams of dried juniper needles and bury most of them in a small pot of soil. Sprinkle the remaining needles on top of the soil and place the pot in the room where most of the ghostly activity is.

JASMINE

Jasminum officinale

Being a native plant of Kashmir, it was considered a sacred bloom, representing harmony, peace, and spiritual protection in the past.

More recently, it was seen as symbolizing the moon and has been used in spells to generate money and to find a soul mate. Often, it was burnt in the bedroom to induce prophetic dreams. Although jasmine isn't a plant that offers protection from psychic attacks or spirits, it can promote better sleep. If dried jasmine is combined with dried lavender and situated somewhere in the bedroom, they will ward off nighttime demons and offer a peaceful sleep.

KNOTWEED

Fallopia japonica

Although Japanese knotweed is so hardy it will disrupt the fabric and foundation of houses, it is a binding plant that effectively controls someone's actions.

If you believe someone has cursed you, pull up some knotweed and write their name on each leaf. Say this spell three times while wrapping the knotweed around your left hand:

"I bind your strength. I bind your curse. You cannot harm me."

Afterward, leave the weed to dry out for a few weeks and then burn it.

LAVATERA (OR MALLOW)

Malvaceae

Interestingly, lavatera is seen as a plant of two symbolisms. Primarily it is used to stimulate romantic interest and help heal those with a broken heart.

This plant also warns against undue passion and being swept away by love. In days gone by, a few flowers were carried in people's pockets to protect themselves from harmful love spells.

Anyone who casts a spell on another person without their consent affects the recipient's karma. In a round-about way, because a spell can influence a mindset, this kind of magic is believed to be a form of psychic attack. Today, lavatera is used to break a love spell and free the individual from its clutches.

If a person believes they are under some kind of en-chantment, they will light a pink candle beside a cup of the flower heads and say the following twelve times:

"This hex will break with the spell I make.
Magic will release me; magic will set me free."

After the spell has been spoken, close with the words "So mote it be," and let the candle burn down.

Scatter the petals outside on a windy day, and as the wind carries them away, the spell should be broken.

LAVENDER

Lavandula

Lavender has been known as a pacifier and purifier for centuries, encouraging serenity to treat headaches and exhaustion. Herbalists also use this popular herb to calm skin irritations, but it has other medicinal uses and can help with many medical conditions.

Spiritually, it is linked with the crown chakra, so hav-ing its scent around during meditation aids spiritual con-nectivity, achieving a higher purpose.

Magically, lavender is adept at chasing away malevolent spirits and, if worn on the body, will protect someone from the evil eye. To receive its protection in dream sleep, sprinkle a few drops of lavender essential oil on your pillow before you sleep.

MANDRAKE

Mandragora officiarum

Made famous in the Harry Potter books, mandrake has been used since ancient times, and it does come with a warning: Never eat it because it is highly toxic, and try not to get it on your skin as it might irritate. Despite it being poisonous, it has psychoactive properties; shamans used it to aid connection to other worlds, and the Ancient Greeks used it more practically as an anesthetic. Folklore says when it is pulled from the earth, it screams and the sound can be fatal to human beings. Mandrake amplifies all other protective herbs, so seeing it on a witch's altar is common. Placing a small amount in a locket and wearing it will protect you from any evil spirits.

MUGWORT (THE MOTHER HERB)

Artemisia vulgaris

Tradition has it that mugwort was once known as the witch's herb and was more appropriately labeled as "cronewort" by some. It was usually left by the door of the neighborhood witch, healer, or midwife. This magical plant is renowned for protecting its keeper and can keep out evil spirits if dried and scattered underneath a doormat. Some people who believe they have been possessed drink it as tea, which is thought to cleanse the soul.

MUGWORT AND VINEGAR

Many spells and rituals call for the use of vinegar when banishing evil spirits or removing a haunting. It can interfere with magic, prevent the manifestation of ghosts and spirits, and keep demons at bay.

To bind the power of a spirit, pour some vinegar on a plate and scatter about a tablespoon of mugwort over the top. Leave the dish in situ for a week. The combination of mugwort and vinegar will silence the spirit and stop it from harassing the residents.

NASTURTIUM

Tropaeolum

In past times, nasturtium was eaten to treat bronchitis or other chest and throat conditions, or applied to wounds to fight infection. Regarding spirituality, it was believed that consuming these plants would enhance psychic perception, banish fear, and boost confidence. When a house is haunted, the occupants will naturally be terrified, and the spirit will feed off that fear, making it stronger and more troublesome. Eating the flowers of this plant will empower you with courage and give you the upper hand. You can also steep the flowers in boiling water and drink the elixir.

NETTLE

Urtica

Despite the unpleasant sting a nettle can give you when you brush past it by accident, the people of old saw it as a beneficial healing plant. Generally, nettle tea, with its anti-inflammatory and analgesic properties, was drunk to reduce arthritic swelling. It was also used in spells and rituals to combat male infertility, which might have resulted from a curse or some form of black magic. Witches also believe this plant will catch a curse and return it to its sender.

If you think you are the victim of a curse, hex, or the evil eye, you must prepare the nettle by removing the leaves (wear gloves), and blanching them in boiling water.

Cooking will remove the fine hairs that contain the sting. Eat a cup of cooked nettles every day for a week, and the curse should be lifted.

ONION

Allium capa

The Ancient Egyptians considered the internal ring structure of the onion to represent eternal life. For this reason, many pharaohs were buried with onions to ward off evil spirits.

More recently, chopping an onion in half has become customary to ward off evil spirits, leaving the cut side facing up. Additionally, placing a peeled garlic clove on top of the chopped onion could increase the magic. Scallions can be grown in pots, gardens, or balconies to expel evil and prevent it from invading the home.

OREGANO

Origanum vulgare

This popular herb is steeped in history and superstition. The name is said to have originated with the Ancient Greeks, who called it the "joy of the mountains," probably because it grows in abundance in the wild. They also believed that if oregano grew on top of a grave, their loved ones would find happiness in the afterlife. Many practitioners today purposely grow it in their gardens to remove any negative vibrations and sometimes keep small pots on their windowsills to protect the home from evil.

PLANTAIN

Plantago

For years, the Caribbean people used the crushed leaves of a plantain to treat inflamed skin and dermatitis. Eating plantains was also thought to lift depression. On a magical level, placing plantains under the pillow while sleeping will drive away evil spirits and prevent night terrors.

PARSLEY

Petroselinum crispum

This herb dates to Ancient Greece and Rome and, in many cultures, is associated with Persephone and death. In past times, it was often present at funerals and seen as a wreath that decorated graves and tombs. Parsley is said to take a long time to germinate since the seeds need to travel to the underworld and return to grow.

Today, magical practitioners still use this herb to contact the dead for protection. One ancient method of ensuring your property is free from ghosts and spirits is by pushing some parsley into the cracks of an outer wall. Alternatively, you can make tea using holy water and parsley to undo a curse.

ROSEMARY

Salvia rosimarinus

For centuries this herb has been used in food and made into a tonic for the central nervous system, helping the person to grow mental strength.

Spiritually, it is seen to be helpful for memory and increasing intuition while aiding psychic protection. In folklore, rosemary has associations with witches, warlocks, and fairies. It was also coveted at weddings and funerals. The mourners would hold bunches of it or wear a sprig on their clothes as a sign of respect, believing it would protect the corpse from evil intentions.

Rosemary incense is widely used in spiritual circles today to cleanse areas and eliminate negative spirits. If your house isn't haunted, you can burn a stick once a week to ensure that a ghost won't take up residence. If spirits plague your home, you may need to light an incense stick daily and use it alongside other powerful methods in this chapter.

ROWAN

Sorbus aucuparia

Often called the "tree of life" or "mountain ash," it is revered by many traditions. The Celts said it brought courage and protection. Scottish tradition said the rowan tree protected its owner from enchantment and black magic, especially if its berries were prolific and bright red. Similarly, fairy lore says that rowan works against evil spirits.

Even today, most white witches will grow a rowan tree in their garden as it is said to ward off sinister warlocks and the evil eye. If you move to a new property and see a rowan tree growing, it's a safe bet that the house is free from evil.

SAGE

Salvia

This powerful aromatic herb has been in use since Roman times. Sage is burnt to cleanse and heal any harmful energy buildup that has accrued over time. Its name derives from the Latin verb to heal. Smudging houses to purify them of evil intent comes top of the list, and some people will use a sage smudging stick regularly for the best effect. These are easy to purchase online.

Some believe that to rid a home of negativity you must use the white variety of sage, but it is a more common thought that any variety will work just as well.

SPANISH MOSS

Tillandsia useneoides

This beautiful long-hanging plant attaches itself to the trees around the countries of the Caribbean and is essential to the ecosystem. Often it will be prolific around swamps, such as in Louisiana. It is used in many hoodoo and voodoo rituals to encourage love or to exact revenge on an unfaithful lover. Spanish moss can also dispel negativity and release long-term blockages in other traditions. The Native Americans called it "Spanish beard" after the Spanish conquistadors.

Hanging this plant in a pot up high near a window will deter any undesirable energies lingering in your home.

TANSY

Tanacetum vulgare

This attractive plant is bright yellow and grows in clusters. It is an aid to differing health problems, and often establishes itself in the wild. Gardeners find the plant helpful in getting rid of pests. Historically it is known as a magical plant, possessing protective abilities, warding off malevolent entities, and casting out witches. Also, it is used to aid divination by enhancing psychic ability and promoting prophetic dreams.

One belief today is that it can help protect animals and surround them in protection. If you have a spirit in your home, place some dried tansy in a bowl and leave it in the same room where the pet sleeps; this should divert the ghost away.

THYME

Thymus vulgaris

For centuries thyme has been used to encourage purification and healing. It is thought to cleanse the mind and body, at the same time protecting against negative energy. Thyme was also said to aid communication with fairies and the deceased. Ancients would stuff their pillows with this herb to prevent psychic attacks in dream sleep.

Grow some thyme in a pot outside, and when it has matured and is ready for picking, cut off around ten strong twigs and tie them in a bunch with some string.

Hang a bunch of thyme in every window in the home to ensure evil doesn't enter.

URN PLANT

Aechmea fasciata

Also known as a bromeliad plant, its silver foliage with a stunning pink blossom in the central part can be toxic. Grown mainly in South American rainforests, this plant is valued by local tribes who attribute its ability to enhance clarity and focus by creating purity and strength within the mind and body. It was said to give powerful psychic protection if grown around one's property or taken into the home.

VERBENA (VERVAIN)

Verbena bonaniensis

This plant has clusters of small starry flowers that come in various colors; the blossoms are fragrant and popular with gardeners worldwide. Verbena's spiritual meanings are sadness and healing, but this has not stopped many cultures from using it to bless buildings and altars against sinister predators or the evil eye. The Ancient Romans thought the plant sacred, and it was called the "tears of Isis."

It was said to be used to summon supernatural forces to gain power over others. For those who are visited at night by vampire-type creatures, sleep with a few sprigs of vervain under your pillow.

VIBURNUM

Opulus

A scented and pretty plant with clusters of flowers. Viburnum is said to aid connection to the angelic realm and represents innocence, purity, and calmness. In Ukraine, viburnum adopts a special significance; they see it as representing not only girls, love, and motherhood, but, most important, the soul of their nation. When wanting to connect with the angelic and elemental guardians for personal protection, this plant would have been used in ancient times to enhance the protective powers of a specific place.

WILLOW TREE

Salix

Willow is purported to have feminine energy, and Native Americans would take branches from the willow and tie them to their canoes to bring protection against evil spirits and drowning. Many witches today have wands made from willow wood as a powerful tool to ward off sinister magic and malicious intent.

To cast out evil spirits from a property, find a willow tree in the neighborhood and, before you break off a small twig or branch, touch the bark and ask the tree's permission to use its power. Take the stick home and decorate it in any way you like, with ribbons or crystal chips. Go into every room in the house, point the wand at the ceiling, and demand the spirit to leave. By keeping it somewhere on show, it should dissuade any spirit from setting up residence in your house, and any ghosts already present in the home will leave.

WISTERIA

Chinensis

When in full bloom, wisteria is stunning with white or lavender cascades, but the pods are toxic and not to be ingested. Folklore tells us that demons and sprites give the vine a wide berth because it is poisonous to them. This woody vine can grow as tall as sixty feet and is often trained to grow over doorways; this is supposed to ward off the evil eye, and the property owners assume they will be kept safe. If you are fortunate enough to have a garden, grow a wisteria tree near the walls of your home for everlasting protection.

YEW

Taxus baccata

Numerous cultures associate the yew tree with death; hence, many of them are grown in graveyards to protect the corpses from grave robbers and to ward off sinister magic. Druids were said to add yew clippings to the coffin to preserve the body for the afterlife.

The Celtic religions recognized the yew as symbolizing death and rebirth; when Christianity became more prevalent, it took on another slant, meaning death and resurrection.

Folklore tells us that one of the reasons it was planted in graveyards is because it was believed the tree would capture the spirits of the dead and prevent them from haunting.

YUCCA

Yucca symbolizes loyalty, healing, protection, and purity and is believed to aid the spiritual journey toward enlightenment by clarifying one's thinking. If grown in the garden at home or brought indoors, it is purported to be like a guardian plant for the family and will ward off anything spiritually harmful. As the yucca tree has many healing properties, it is also said to help keep illnesses at bay.

ZEBRA

Calathea zebrina

This beautiful green-and-white variegated plant has much to offer in the home as it is said to help communication with one's guide, which should bring empowerment and closure to long-lasting problems. It is also known as an

air purifier, and it is believed to be able to cleanse negative vibrations. The larger these plants grow, the more
protection they offer.

CRYSTALS FOR PROTECTION

SINCE ANCIENT TIMES, PEOPLE HAVE used crystals to tap
into their power. These potent stones can be used for a variety of
different things, including health and well-being, magic spells,
and, ultimately, protection.

Because there are hundreds of crystal types, knowing which to
use for particular situations can be challenging. In this chapter,
we will only discuss the most effective ones in defending against
ghostly or demonic issues, and look at how to combine the energy
of multiple crystals to boost their power.

All the items on the list below have the ability to protect a
person from psychic or physical attack, but as you will see, some
may perform better than others. As a result, even though you can
use all of the items for the same purpose, some are much more
effective at driving away ghosts and demons, while others would
be more successful at providing protection against curses or the
evil eye.

When you come to purchase a crystal, it is usually best to get
a feel for it before you bring it home. Sometimes a stone will feel

hot or cold in your hand, or you may sense it giving off an energy or charge. These are all good signs that your crystal is active. Even the smallest of stones, like beads or chips, will still work, so if you want around-the-clock protection, you should purchase some crystal jewelry that you can wear regularly.

CRYSTAL CARE

BEFORE YOU decide to use your crystals, taking care of them is crucial. Each one must be prepared beforehand with a blessing and cleansing. Before it reaches you, it's likely to have been handled by many people. For example, think about how it was obtained from the ground, the factory packers, and the individuals who deliver it to the stores or online for sale. Every person has a unique vibration, some positive and others negative. The stone will absorb the energy from everyone who has touched it, so it's your job to purify and rid it of any unwanted vibes so that it can work best for you.

CLEANSING

THERE ARE a few ways to cleanse a crystal. First, you must find out if your chosen stone is porous; if it is, you are best to perform a dry cleanse. Take a large bowl of household salt, bury the crystal completely, and leave it overnight. Another method is to leave the stone outside on a dry night on a full moon phase. The power from the moon will not only cleanse it but will charge and empower it.

For hardier, nonporous stones, collect some rainwater in a bowl, preferably on a full or new moon phase, and soak the stone overnight. The following day, use a kitchen towel to dry it thoroughly. Another quick and easy way to cleanse is to trail the smoke of an incense stick over the crystal for a few minutes. Sage or dragon's blood is most favorable, or any of the below.

LAVENDER, PALO SANTO, SANDALWOOD, CEDAR, PINE, SAGE, JASMINE, EUCALYPTUS

While you are smudging your crystal, repeat this mantra a few times:

"I cleanse this stone of all things impure.
I bathe this crystal in positive light."

Many witches and shamans who use crystals in their craft like to sleep with the stone under their pillow for a few nights, so it absorbs the owner's vibration.

ENERGIZE

ONCE THE crystal is free of any contaminated energy, it's time to empower it. Sit quietly in a room, holding your stone in both hands. Imagine a light coming directly from your face while staring at the stone. Think about how you want it to work for you.

In this case, you would ask for protection, so visualize the stone's magic radiating toward you, encircling you in a bright light. You can think about your problem and speak to the crystal directly, asking it to help.

After ten minutes, you can end the ritual by saying the following:

"Lend me your power and shield me.
Surround me in light, so bright."

Every time a new situation springs up where you need the crystal's power, cleanse and empower it again using the same method. Imagine it's like a cell phone and charge it up regularly.

It's never a good idea to allow others to touch your crystals unless you are performing some healing. If someone needs to hold it, re-cleanse and energize it before it can work again for you.

When a crystal is ready to take action, you can harness its power in a few different ways. Nestling it under your pillow or resting it on a nightstand will defend you at night. For daytime protection, make sure you are always carrying it on your person. If you are using a small tumble stone, for example, keep it in your pocket, or ladies can slip it inside their bra. An excellent way to ensure it is always with you is to purchase a crystal in jewelry form. A necklace, bracelet, ring, or earring can work just as well as a single stone, but be sure to treat them in the same way by cleansing and empowering them beforehand.

Sometimes, if your situation is dire, you can carry a combination of stones for added power.

AMETHYST

Color: deep or pale purple

This lavender or deep purple crystal is one of the most potent and protective stones and will guard against most psychic attacks. It blends well when used in conjunction with other protective stones like chlorite, and has many healing properties. Amethyst also helps with insomnia, so if demonic forces target you at night, it will protect you and induce peaceful sleep so you can rest.

AMETRINE

Color: combination of purple and yellow

In shades of yellow and lavender, this crystal is twinned with citrine and amethyst, making it a powerful combination of instant action. It is used for meditation and astral travel and will ward off any psychic attacks when the soul is not earthbound. As it is such an energetic crystal, it can revitalize a person exhausted by life or worn down by negativity.

BERYL

Color: blue, golden, pink, white, and green

This stone was often used for scrying, which is believed to be how the crystal ball was born. Many witches, soothsayers, and psychics revere the power of beryl. Golden beryl aids all magical workings and gives its owner the courage to seek out forbidden realms or experiences. It is also known to protect against unseen forces, evil spirits, and negative energy and helps the novice be more adventurous in gaining psychic experiences.

BLOODSTONE

Color: dark green and red

A green quartz with reddish and greenish tints is said to ward off evil and have weather-controlling powers, mainly when used in conjunction with magic. It senses when psychic danger is approaching and can redirect it away from the owner so if you think someone has cast the evil eye, this would be one of the stones to choose. The Ancient Egyptians used this crystal to shrink tumors and cleanse the blood. It has numerous healing properties and is valuable to any crystal collection.

CHLORITE

Color: pale green

This pale green crystal is one of the most powerful to ward off psychic attacks, especially when combined with ruby and carnelian. It is a helpful stone for crystal gridding (see page 194) and is known to ease pain. Fall asleep holding this powerful stone in your hand, and you should sleep peacefully from any disruptive psychic attacks.

CARNELIAN

Color: orange, red, or brown

In the past, it was used to aid and protect a deceased person on their journey to the afterlife; today, it's believed to invigorate other stones in its vicinity.

A piece of raw carnelian would be placed by the front and back doors of properties to ward off evil spirits and to bring abundance and prosperity to the family. It has numerous healing properties and is respected for its powerful protection against the unknown.

DANBURITE

Color: lilac, pink, white, and yellow

This crystal is delicate and ethereal, with a pure vibration, drawing enlightenment to its owner. An excellent stone to place near a very sick or dying person in a hospital, as it protects them in their weakened state from any psychic intrusion. If a loved one is at the end of their life, place a piece of danburite in their hand and when they finally pass away, keep the crystal inside the coffin.

DOLOMITE

Color: pink and gray

Dolomite is a tabular crystal known as dolomite rock, and is easily sourced. If purchased in the raw state, it would be a good idea to store it in a drawstring bag as it can be easily scratched. This crystal is often used for infants as a nighttime protector against nightmares. It is said to soothe children frightened of the dark or to protect them against any otherworldly presence in their room. As the crystal is fragile, placing it somewhere out of reach would be wise.

EMERALD

Color: green and opaque green

In past times this beautiful gemstone was known to predict future events when held in the hand. In ancient folklore, it was said to have strong powers of protection against magicians, evil witches, and warlocks. It is recommended not to wear this gemstone continuously as it may activate negative thoughts.

EPIDOTE

Color: pistachio green and rust

Epidote needs careful handling and firm instructions from the owner as to what is required. It can magnify both good and bad vibrations, so take care, as it is not a stone for a newbie or novice. This crystal can be used as an after-healing energy, if someone is recovering from a psychic attack or is very worn down. In that case, it can re-attune the person's energy levels to normality and bring excellent soul growth when dealing with adverse situations.

FLUORITE

Color: clear, green, purple, and brown

This beautiful crystal may be a little expensive, but it is highly protective and versatile on a psychic level. When worn, it will repel any negative energy away from the wearer, so it is excellent if around miserable or negative people. It also protects IT equipment from virus attacks, so a small piece near the computer should be helpful. As it absorbs undesirable energies and fends off psychic intrusions, it is recommended to cleanse any fluorite crystals daily, smudging with dragon's blood or white sage incense.

GARNET

Color: deep red, pink, orange, yellow, and black

Sometimes known as the gem of faith, this beautiful crystal was worn as a talisman to ward off sinister entities and the evil eye in times gone by. If a person did good deeds for others, then more benefits would come to them, but if their behavior was inappropriate when wearing a garnet, its protection was lost, and ill fortune was said to dog them. This gemstone is said to restore harmony when a psychic crisis exists around a home or individual.

GABBRO

Color: black, gray, and white

This stone is a plutonic igneous rock and created when molten rock solidifies. It is said to be found on the moon, Mars, Earth, and large asteroids. In recent years gabbro has become known for its mystical powers and ability to clear dense energy blockages and generate an extensive shield of protection around the user. It dispels undesirable psychic debris from them and creates spiritual love and guidance against sinister intent.

HERKIMER DIAMOND

Color: clear

In ancient times Hindus strongly believed that the vibrations of double-terminated quartz crystals emitted a very positive aura to many organs in the body. Other healing powers attributed to Herkimer diamonds are protection for the owner and its ability to disperse bad dreams, night terrors, and visiting demons. It has power to dispel electromagnetic pollution and, after gridding the house and beds, will ward off negativity.

IRON PYRITE

Color: brownish gold

Iron pyrite has an excellent energy field, especially when blocking out sinister vibrations. Worn as a pendant or bracelet, it protects the owner from psychic attacks and demonic spiritual bodies. If a person is filled with deep despair, it weakens them and opens up portals to ill intent; this crystal becomes aware of this and goes into action to redirect the undesirable energy.

IDOCRASE

Color: olive green, pale blue, and red

Idocrase is an excellent releasing crystal that helps to heal past hurts, even going back to other incarnations. If a person unknowingly has been taken over by an entity, it can be exhausting, making them feel they are a prisoner in their own body. Idocrase helps to repair and disperse negativity, allowing the person to become free.

JADE

Color: many shades of green

Jade is a protective stone that guards the wearer from being the victim of black magic or being cursed. It is prized in the East and has been used throughout time as an amulet for safety. The ancients would place the crystal on their third eye to promote dream sleep premonitions and to awaken psychic ability.

JASPER

Color: red, brown, green, and purple

Jasper is commonly used to align the chakras, and it is said to clear electromagnetic density and environmental pollution. In past times the shamans used jasper to protect them from unseen forces when they went into a trance, venturing on their spiritual journeys to gain psychic information. To discourage negative spirits from entering their space, many psychics today will have this crystal resting beside them when they perform readings.

KYANITE

Color: white, blue, pink, green, yellow, and black

This versatile psychic crystal is beneficial in so many ways. Meditation and attunement can also allow spiritual energy to manifest into thought, so focusing on protection will shield the owner. As it does not attract negativity, this is one of those crystals that shouldn't need cleansing. In cases where a person is about to pass away, kyanite will aid with the transition, ensuring that the patient is protected until they reach their ultimate destination.

KUNZITE

Color: yellow, pink, clear, and lavender

Kunzite, a very spiritual crystal, comes in a variety of colors. It has an elevated vibration and can strongly aid otherworldly meditations. Not only does it protect an individual, but it also cleanses the environment they live in. Its protective sheath will dispel any evil entities attached to a person and clear up any sinister debris.

LABRADORITE

Color: iridescent blue, black, and yellow

This beautiful and mystical crystal will often give the appearance of changing its colors when seen in different lights. The stone brings light with solid protection for the wearer, raising psychic awareness and universal healing energy. It promotes intuition for novices and helps them attain their spiritual pathway while ensuring their safety when assisting their soul for spiritual ascension.

LAPIS LAZULI

Color: deep blue with flecks of gold

Lapis lazuli is the key to spiritual attainment. It has the ability to know when its owner is under psychic attack and is said to contact the person's angel or guide for assistance. Ancient Egyptians revered this crystal and adorned their jewelry and artifacts with gemstones to gain spiritual protection.

MERLINITE

Color: black and white

This unassuming crystal is indeed powerful and said to hold many hidden secrets. It is used mainly by shamans, priests, magicians, and witches for magical rituals and rites. It aids astral travel and allows access to the Akashic records, both past and present. Merlinite is a safety belt for universal travel, ensuring the traveler will return safely from adventures on the astral plane. Keep a piece under your pillow if you intend to scoot about the ether.

MOLDAVITE

Color: bottle green

Moldavite is probably the most powerful of crystals and is rare, which might explain why it's so expensive. It is said to have extraterrestrial origins, and came to Earth as a meteorite between Romania and Ukraine in Moldova. It also magnifies other crystals in its vicinity, boosting their vibrational powers. Psychic people who wear it can often feel nauseous or lightheaded before they get used to it. As it can enhance psychic ability, they may find themselves experiencing prophetic dreams. It can download knowledge from the Akashic records to the wearer, revealing past and future lives to come. For those linking to the ascended masters through meditation, moldavite should keep you safe from anything sinister on that journey.

NATROLITE

Color: white, pink, and pale lemon

Natrolite stimulates the third-eye chakra to open and aids in developing various psychic skills. This stone is claimed to serve as a purifier when submerged in water for a short period. The water can then be put into a spray bottle to clear haunted locations and drive away demons. White witches may spray their altars before casting spells, spraying directly onto people who have experienced break-ins or altered sleep patterns.

NUUMMITE

Color: speckled black

Known as the Sorcerer's Stone and discovered in Greenland, this crystal is ancient and a powerful talisman that forms a barrier against negative energies, protecting the wearer from black magic, demons, and witchcraft. It is also beneficial against cursing and the evil eye. It is purported to cleanse one's aura with purifying energy and disperse the harmful debris buildup accumulated around one's etheric body, thus conveying feelings of well-being.

OBSIDIAN

Color: black, mahogany, electric blue, green, gold sheen, and brown

Obsidian is formed from molten lava and is one of the most powerful protective crystals. It is a formidable asset when spell casting and healing, and can shield a person from demonic forces. It strips away deception to bring the truth to the surface and urges the owner to grow their soul and progress from childish limitations to an adult understanding of all that is divine and spiritual. It will block psychic attacks and cleanse any negative energies around most people. Black or mahogany obsidian is best suited for this task. It is a good idea to cleanse this crystal daily as it is superfast to absorb any negative energy. Rinse in tepid water, place it out in the rain, or just let the cold tap rinse it.

OKENITE

Color: white or pale blue and yellow

Okenite is a colorless silicate mineral whose structure resembles small furry snowballs. As it's so tactile and pretty, it is a crystal favored in these New Age times. It brings the completion of harsh karmic lessons, enabling the owner to walk away from the destructive energies of times gone by. Okenite is ideal for opening the way for trance channeling. It ensures solid spiritual protection around a person, enabling them to feel safe from any destructive vibrations while connecting with other worlds.

PERIDOT

Color: bright green, olive green, yellow, and red-brown

The mineral peridot is a beautiful crystal that provides joy and light into one's life. The Egyptians highly prized it and used it to create jewelry and antiques. Peridot has been used for centuries to fend off evil spirits and the evil eye and is thought to act as a sleep aid, preventing nightmares and night terrors. A crystal that is ideal for healers, it has numerous qualities that can treat multiple bodily ailments.

PETALITE

Color: white, pink, gray, clear, and green

Petalite is a lithium aluminum silicate. A crystal favored in New Age circles and gaining tremendous popularity, it is also known as the Angel Stone to assist in angelic connection when meditating. Shamans treasure this crystal as it offers protection when setting out for a vision quest or journeying to other realms. Clear petalite is often selected for this reason.

QUARTZ

Color: clear and various colors

Clear quartz is sometimes referred to as the Universal Crystal. It can be striated, elongated, or in clusters. It is said to be the most powerful of all crystals as it has multipurpose attributes such as storing, adapting, absorbing, and releasing energy, not to mention being a master healer. Crystal collectors often purchase a large chunk of clear quartz and place other crystals on top to energize them; this magnifies their powers significantly.

All quartz crystals protect most things, so if you doubt which crystal to use, this will always be suitable.

TANGERINE QUARTZ

Color: orange

It is helpful in aiding a person who has been shocked or distressed by a psychic attack. Often, mediums will use this for soul retrieval work.

ROSE QUARTZ

Color: pink

This beautiful pink crystal is loved by all and is very good for soothing children who are ill or scared to go to bed at night. Put a chunk of it beside their bed for protection or a tumble stone under their pillow.

RUTILATED QUARTZ (ANGEL HAIR)

Color: golden, brown, and clear

Rutilated quartz has fine striations within it resembling hair, and is used as a vibrational healer. It aids in scrying, astral travel, and channeling, especially to the angelic or alien realms. It protects healers and therapists when dealing with clients who have come under psychic attack and will break down any negativity for the victim.

RUBY

Color: red

This crystal is all-powerful and extremely beautiful, encouraging the wearer to follow their bliss. This stone is a powerhouse against psychic attack and will enable the owner to be more assertive in verbal debate and stand up for oneself, especially in anything legal.

SELENITE

Color: white, brown, green, and orange

Selenite is a perfect ethereal crystal for all spiritual work, bringing calmness and coolness to its wearer. Often used as a wand, it's helpful in gridding a house or a bed and putting in strong powers of protection. When confronting demons, some mediums will use selenite to cut the negative tentacle energy that clings to people, thus freeing them from their trauma. Mediums will also use a selenite wand to close harmful entrance portals and stop unwanted entities from entering the Earth plane.

SERAPHINITE

Color: green

The darker stones of this crystal have small silvery feathers in their layers, and so are sometimes linked with the angels and spiritual enlightenment. When meditating with this, the soul is said to ascend to a higher vibration and travel on out-of-body journeys. Seraphinite protects the physical body from psychic attack until the soul returns to base.

TIGER'S EYE

Color: brown and yellow

This brown and yellow crystal places a powerful barrier around its owner, defending against any evil intent or psychic attack. It is probably the most recognized for being the go-to stone when dealing with any supernatural problem. It protects against cursing and spite or people who are being vindictive. It enhances psychic abilities and encourages the kundalini if placed on the third-eye chakra.

TOURMALINE

Color: black

Tourmaline is a strong grounding crystal, especially if the chakras are out of alignment. Used in shamanic rituals, it gives protection to cleanse negative energy and purify the aura, mainly if the person has encountered the evil eye or has been verbally or physically mistreated. Black tourmaline will benefit the owner at night, ensuring they don't venture onto the negative astral plane.

CRYSTALS FOR CHILDREN

MOST CHILDREN ARE PSYCHIC UNTIL the age of seven, as they are still close to the spirit realms, especially when they are babies and toddlers. Many infants give off powerful energy and can be targeted by lower entities such as shadow people and disincarnate souls who feed on the child's purity. Sadly, many children can visibly see these creatures, and when they show fear, they generate even more energy that the spirit will cling to.

Today's little ones are fascinated by crystals, so you should let them choose a few tumbled stones if you go to a crystal shop. Some pretty little gemstone bracelets might appeal to them as well.

The crystals below are perfect for children and are best placed in the child's bedroom. For infants and toddlers, you can situate them somewhere out of reach so they avoid swallowing them, and for older children, they can have them beside their bed or carry them in their school bag.

Rose quartz represents pure love and can block evil vibrations.

Carnelian has many healing properties but can ward off any psychic misuse directed at the infant.

Prehnite is a lime-green crystal and originates from South Africa and is said to connect with the powerful healing angel Raphael. It has a protective field that shields the child against anything evil.

Amethyst is a favorite with children and a calming stone that promotes sleep quality and reduces nightmares.

Tiger's eye not only protects the child from sinister entities, but it also helps to give them courage.

GRIDDING THE BED

The darkest hour is just before dawn.

WHEN A PERSON IS UNDER psychic attack at night, it can be very alarming. Demons, ghosts, and sinister specters love the small hours to terrify their victims. As we have established in earlier chapters, human fear brings power to any form of entity that can manifest into malevolent intent, which can be nearly impossible to remove.

We also spend a third of our time in bed, which is when we are most vulnerable; yet, by "gridding the bed," we can ward off evil spirits.

Place four tourmaline tumble stones under each corner of the bed or under your mattress with four pieces of carnelian. Add green chlorite at the four corners and a piece of amethyst and rose quartz in the center to enhance the power. Ensure you cleanse and empower them beforehand and remove them every few months for another cleansing ritual. The collective power of these stones will create protective energy around you when you are sleeping.

PET PROTECTION

OFTEN, WE FORGET THAT OUR pets need protection against psychic attacks, especially when they live in haunted houses or where poltergeist activity occurs. Because animals are intuitive creatures, they can sense malevolent entities and become terrified, especially dogs and cats because they are highly sensitive. It isn't just evil spirits that we need to shield them from, either. Some will be unfortunate to come in direct contact with people who have evil souls and might harm them. In our area, many cats have been stolen for dog baiting and are thrown into a ring with them to suffer a cruel death; this will feed the evil attached to the people who perpetrate this activity. Many beloved dogs have gone missing, too, and often will never be seen again. Some people believe that when someone kills an animal for pleasure or shows no compassion for them, they might have a demon residing within them, goading them into inhuman conduct. As the demon becomes more robust, it can control the animal killer and encourage them to go on to the heinous act of murdering a human being.

GRIDDING A PET'S BED

ROSE QUARTZ, angelite, amethyst, and sugilite are crystals for protecting an animal. Tumble stones can be placed individually into small drawstring bags and sewn around the bottom or the outside of the pet's bed.

Alternatively, a cylindrical barrel can be filled with selected crystal chips and attached to their collar.

VOGEL WAND

VOGEL WANDS ARE NOT FOR the amateur, and a crystal specialist must train you to use one correctly. Specific angles are cut into the sides of a quartz wand to enhance power and give direction for maximum effect. The broader end of the wand is classed as feminine, drawing pranic energy in, which is made more robust as it spirals through the surfaces. The narrower end is masculine, transmitting a laser-type beam, removing blockages, negativity, and unsettling atmospheres that might develop into malevolent energy.

CALLING ON GUIDES AND ANGELS

MANY PEOPLE DON'T REALIZE THEY have a spirit guide walking beside them throughout their life. As we have touched on in a previous chapter, it doesn't matter what faith you ascribe to or even if you have no belief in religion at all. Every time we reincarnate onto the Earth plane, we don't come alone; a guide is usually in situ and will support us throughout our journey.

It is believed that small children and babies can physically see their guides until they reach the age of about five to seven years. They can also see spirits and ghosts, probably because their soul is renewed and hasn't been affected by earthly influences.

It's common for little children to have imaginary friends, but who can say they aren't real? Often, a guide will change their appearance to mimic an infant, helping the youngster adjust to life and settle into their new world.

CASE STUDY: LEANNA
ERIK

I was one of those children who had an imaginary friend. He was a young boy, the same age as me, and his name was Erik. He had a shock of blond hair and bright blue eyes, and he would mainly sit on my bed at night and talk to me about all kinds of things. I can't recall the conversations ever being spiritual. Usually, they were about my day and what was happening at school, and sometimes he would tell me about things that would happen, like my friend falling off her bike. On one occasion, he came to me in a dream and told me my parents wouldn't stay together and that I had another man to help raise me. When I relayed this information to my mother, she was shocked, but after a few years, she divorced my father and married my now stepfather.

I suffered from ear infections a lot as a child, and on numerous occasions, when I was crying or in pain, Erik would place both his hands on my ears and heal me. As I grew up, so did he until I reached puberty, and he gradually became invisible. It was strange, though, because I knew he was still there even though I didn't see him anymore. I later found out Erik was, in fact, my guide and remained visible to me until I became an adult.

It is said we have known our guides forever. They live as people on the Earth plane, repeating the reincarnation process until they have experienced most of life's lessons firsthand. We have to understand that guides are not angels, so even though they are highly evolved, they are not perfect, but they have a profound understanding of life and how best to help us work through our problems.

Some guides will even reincarnate with their subject and play an active role in a person's life. These guides are known as earth avatars and will assist us in becoming wonderful friends. Because they are in a more advanced state than us, their role is to help a person achieve the very best within themselves and to get off the karmic wheel of reincarnation.

Every person walking the earth has at least one of these divine beings, and although they're invisible to the human eye, they interact with us daily through our subconscious. Our guides are powerful and can influence certain situations we might find ourselves in, but because many life lessons we encounter are preplanned and put in place for our spiritual development, they will only help us if they are allowed.

Psychic attacks, amongst other supernatural happenings, are never preordained. Sometimes, accidentally, we can stumble into the presence of a predator, be it human or spiritual, and because this was never the plan, our guides can often assist and protect us from harm.

How many guides have we?

It is believed there can be as many as twenty or thirty guides for each person, and they are put in place to refine the structures of our personalities. One guide could inspire a creative gift within a person; another might help with shyness or assertiveness. If there are flaws within an individual's personality, a specific spirit helper will be on hand to fine-tune their qualities and bring out the very best in them. Being authors, sometimes when we are writing, we feel a literary guide around us, and if we suffer temporarily from writer's block, by simply asking them to help, new inspiration will suddenly materialize.

Each of us has a primary guide, one who is with us throughout all our incarnations, but others who specialize in specific issues can be brought in to assist briefly. Like Erik above, there are guides to ease us into life and support us while we are children, but often when we reach adulthood, our primary guide takes over.

In our life plan, we will be asked to undergo difficult lessons, such as experiencing the death of a loved one, extreme health issues, or even mental illnesses. By undergoing these challenging situations firsthand, we are growing the soul and gaining proper understanding. One saying is "You cannot teach what you haven't learned." Although we might feel beleaguered at times when dealing with such challenging and complex life lessons, each step of the way, we are given a helping hand to smooth the journey. Hopefully, the young soul will burgeon into a wiser soul when it returns to the spirit world. We have to remember that we are not here to become too involved in someone else's game plan because it restricts the reason for our lessons and existence. By seeking a guide's assistance and protection, we can stay on route and find value in the new things we experience.

GUIDE COMMUNICATION

BECAUSE GUIDES DON'T APPEAR BEFORE you in a puff of smoke, they might communicate with you by sending you signs. It could even be a slogan on the back of a truck on the highway that says something like "Life is for Living!" Perhaps a warning will be given at another time to make a person aware to take care on a particular day. Because a guide frequently communicates with our subconscious mind, paying attention to your inner voice and trusting your intuition are essential. When you wake up in the morning, you might get a bad feeling and decide not to carry out your plans for the day; this might be because your guide has warned you about an unpleasant event you might get caught up in. Also, because it's easier to talk to you directly when you are in an altered state of consciousness, they can appear in your dreams, giving you relevant information or showing you an event that might take place. It's best to develop the skill of being alert to the small signs in life that can hold a profound revelation.

INTERCEDING GUIDES

OFTEN, A GUIDE WILL STEP in to help their protégé by using someone else, especially if the person is at rock bottom and psychically unable to receive information. It could be a clairvoyant, a medium, a friend, or just a sentence that jumps out of a presenter's mouth on the television. When stressed out, a person creates psychic static, which interferes with the choices that must be made. A better form of communication has to be found, so by entering the psyche of a relative or counselor, they might be able to help the individual get back on track. A guide can link in and psychically converse with anyone; an acquaintance or even a passing stranger who happens to be in the same orbit.

FEELING ABANDONED BY YOUR GUIDES

FIRSTLY, YOU ARE NEVER ABANDONED by your spirit helpers however lonely you are, or however much you feel you are being punished. People say, "Why me?" or "What have I done to deserve this? Where are my guides and angels?" In truth, the guides have never left. Whatever is happening in a person's life, however difficult it might be, it will probably be very cathartic in their life plan, especially when karma is being sorted out. It's akin to being in a classroom situation. The guide acts as the tutor, but now the student is left to get on with the exam. Throughout these tests, protection is always in place, maybe even more so than usual, so inner strength must be found to weather the storm and move on from the lesson.

GUIDES FOR OLD AGE

SOMETIMES ALTERNATE GUIDES WILL BE allocated to those becoming elderly and pragmatic or who are filled with sad resignation that there is nothing left to look forward to except, perhaps, death. Because of their bleak state, the elderly can become depressed and difficult to please, and are often in nursing homes or hospitals and feel at their most vulnerable. They will often drift in and out of spiritual realms while sleeping, thus needing special protection from their guides. Usually, the guide will counsel them and prepare them to achieve new skills in crossing over. In this transitional phase of their lives, they can be prone to psychic attacks but are well guarded by their guides to the very end. It's safe to say that it's sometimes daunting and lonely being on planet Earth, but knowing there is a psychic protection plan in place is reassuring and a true blessing.

SHIELDING YOU FROM
PSYCHIC ATTACK

YOU MAY WONDER WHERE A person's guide is if they are being haunted or suffering from a psychic attack. If they are all-powerful and can interject into someone's life, why do so many people get caught up with demonic entities and hostile ghosts? Why are these beings allowed to invade our dreams or pull us out of bed by our feet in the middle of the night? Where is our protection? The truthful answer is we don't know. One theory is that guides are not powerful enough to fight off the strength of a demon; perhaps this is beyond their capabilities, and a more powerful, positive entity, like an angel or archangel, needs to be called upon for assistance. Reports from mediums who work alongside paranormal investigators when clearing ghosts from haunted houses say that even if the spirit has been in limbo for a hundred years, their guide is always present. Sometimes, it takes a living human (the medium) to converse with the ghost and talk them into going toward the light with their guide.

GUARDIAN ANGELS

ANGELS ARE ON A MUCH higher frequency than guides, and certain angels stay with you right through your life, especially in moments of unexpected danger. Spiritual people like to think that our lives are planned and linked to our karmic lessons, but this is only sometimes the case.

MICHAEL, THE ANGEL OF PROTECTION

IN OUR LONG CAREERS AS psychics, we have met many people who claimed to have seen this stunning angel. Long blond hair, piercing blue eyes, and always dressed in pale blue. His size is enormous and can fill a skyline. Mediums or priests will often summon him to rid people of demonic possession or to protect those terrorized in their homes by evil spirits. No entity can match his strength or the power of his flaming sword.

POWER ANIMALS

POWER ANIMALS ARE SPIRITUAL HELPERS that take the form of animals. Originally referred to as totem animals, they are purported to be linked to the Asian and North and South American continents, and many Indigenous tribes will call upon them for protection.

They are valuable companions who assist us while we go through many changes and obstacles in life. You can call upon these wise and reliable creatures for guidance and advice. Regular interaction with them will significantly improve your daily life and broaden your spiritual potential. Every person is said to have a power animal who works solely for them. Often, we might have an affinity with a particular creature, like a wolf or a bird, or we will see a specific creature repeatedly throughout the day. These spiritual beings can also appear to us in dream sleep and make their presence known. They come in many forms, such as tigers, snakes, eagles, stags, bears, etc. They can even be portrayed as mystical beings, like unicorns, dragons, or pegasi.

CASE STUDY: BELETA
BLACK BULLS AND BEARS

I had never really believed in power animals and thought their concept was highly unlikely until, one day, I was making coffee for a friend in my kitchen. She was leaning back casually on the radiator as we chatted. I glanced at her and nearly passed out as an enormous black bear stood robustly beside her. She looked at me and said anxiously, "Are you okay? You look as if you've seen a ghost." When I told her what I had observed, she smiled and remarked excitedly that her power animal was a bear, and she, too, had seen it in her dreams! Some months later, I meditated in bed and asked my animal to reveal itself. I was in a very serene state, with soft music playing, and was concentrating hard on my breathing, when suddenly, a large, ferocious black bull glared down at me. I sat upright, my heart banging through my chest. I couldn't believe what I had just seen! Being quite spiritual, I thought I would have had a beautiful feline or a white stallion, but I had a snorting bull! That night as I settled down to sleep, I dreamed of him, and communicating telepathically, he apologized for frightening me. He said he would tone down his approach and then showed an image of himself as a little calf. It seems we don't always get the animal we would ordinarily choose, but do I believe in them now? You bet!

HOW TO CONNECT TO YOUR POWER ANIMAL

YOU CAN try a sitting meditation, or another good way to connect with a power animal is to do a walking meditation in a forest or wood. If you can manage to camp out, this is even better because being in nature at night strengthens the connection, and witches, especially, believe that doing this on a full moon will guarantee a visit from your spirit animal companion. Find an old tree nearby. Giant oaks are very powerful, or any other tree with large roots at its base. Lean back against the tree and send a message to nature that you want to connect with your power animal. You might not witness it straight away. Sometimes it can take a few days before you are allowed to see them. If you don't receive any messages or visions, it might be that your power animal is more associated with water, so visit the ocean or venture to a brook, lake, or stream and repeat the process.

FIGHTING OFF PSYCHIC ATTACK

JUST AS WE CAN CALL upon angels and guides to protect us when we are being psychically attacked, we can also summon our power animals to do the same. If the problem is demonic, our power animals are particularly useful because often demons are not born from a human soul. In some cultures, for thousands of years cats were considered our spiritual protectors who could sense evil of any kind and ward them off with their presence. Cats, especially, have a dynamic aura known as an astral force, which can repel anything negative. So, if your power animal is any kind of feline, you will be automatically protected.

Sometimes, if an evil entity paralyzes us, our mind is the only part of our body that works. The entity might be able to restrain your movements. Still, it has no control over your will, so silently repeating this phrase, "I summon my power animal to remove this demon, cast it out, send it away," over and over again can often do the trick.

ANIMAL PROTECTION

WE RECOGNIZE THAT ANIMALS CAN psychically tune into and see spirits. Often, dogs can be seen barking at the corners of a room if they live in a haunted location, or cats might hiss at bare spaces and arch their backs. However, sometimes the problem isn't a spirit or ghost but rather an owner affected by a spirit or demon. One theory is that those people who are cruel to animals might have some form of evil inside them. This could be a demonic force that steps in and out of their body at will, or simply that they are just plain evil. The perpetrator may have no power over people, so they will take it out on a vulnerable animal with no voice or strength to fight back. Whether we seek to protect them from psychic attacks or physical assaults, there is a lot we can do to protect these beautiful creatures. Animal lovers who witness cruelty to pets often find this a distressing and heartbreaking scenario, which brings feelings of hopelessness within them. Still, by using the power of the mind, we can create miracles when love and compassion challenge the darker side.

❊ REMEDY FOR ANIMAL PROTECTION ❊

You will need:
A purple cloth
A white tealight candle
Dalmatian jasper
A photo of the animal or one that resembles it
Celestite
Paper and pen
A fireproof bowl

Assemble an altar on a small table and drape a purple cloth over it. Purple is all-powerful and will attract only the highest form of spirit help. Light a white tealight candle and place a piece of Dalmatian jasper crystal on top of a photo of the animal. If you don't have a picture, find one that resembles the animal. The gentle blue celestite crystal is said to be blessed by angelic beings, so hold this in both hands and appeal to the angels of animals to set in place some psychic protection for the creature. Finally, rest this crystal beside the Dalmatian jasper. Write down your personal message of well-being and safety for the animal on a piece of paper, and when the candle has burned halfway down, light the paper from the flame in a fireproof bowl. When the candle has completely burned, take the ashes from the paper and bury them in the ground.

This spell can also be used for getting over the loss of an animal, finding a missing pet, or calming down aggressive children when they are handling animals.

EPILOGUE

PSYCHIC ATTACKS CAN SOMETIMES BE worse than other forms of abuse because these supernatural tormentors are usually invisible to the human eye. Family members may think their loved one is experiencing some sort of mental illness or is going completely insane instead of believing they are being plagued by a ghost or spirit. Parents feel powerless when they cannot defend their children, which makes psychic attacks on youngsters all the more concerning. Even though we lead practical lives, we must keep in mind that just because science hasn't discovered the answers to all of our paranormal encounters doesn't mean that ghosts, demons, or extradimensional creatures aren't real. There have been too many reports of otherworldly activities spanning hundreds of years for us to simply dismiss them as nonsense.

If you have encountered or suffered any of the situations covered in this book, we urge you to step outside the box and try some of our solutions.

In the meantime, we send out positive, protective thoughts to all.

ACKNOWLEDGMENTS

We want to express our gratitude to everyone who helped make this book possible, including our chief editor Joel Fotinos, who trusted us enough to allow us to write this manuscript; our editorial assistant Emily Anderson, who meticulously reviewed every word; and our dependable agent, the late Bill Gladstone, who has had a significant, positive impact on our writing careers over the years.

Additionally, we would like to express our gratitude to Mark Keyes, a paranormal investigator and founder of the Pennsylvania Paranormal Association and author of *Chasing Shadows: A Criminal Investigator's Look into the Paranormal,* and Virginiarose Centrillo, a psychic medium who also works alongside Mark. Thank you so much for sharing your invaluable information with us.

A special thank-you to Louise Chevel. Your experience and vast knowledge of crystals have greatly expanded our understanding of their abilities.

ABOUT THE AUTHORS

My father, Leanna's grandfather, was an American soldier in the Second World War and was posted to a small town in Somerset, England, not far from where my mother lived. She came from a large, happy family and met him at The Fruiters Arms, a pub opposite her home. After a whirlwind romance, they were married, and when I was a year old, we boarded a troop ship to New York to live in Kansas with my father's family. My American grandmother was not only psychic but very shrewd and told my mother, in no uncertain terms, the marriage wouldn't work. At age three, we were back on a ship heading for England, leaving my brokenhearted father behind.

My first spiritual recollection was when I was four. Quite a few of the family were gathered around a large round table, playing the Ouija board, and I watched in fascination as my English grandmother took charge. She, too, was very psychic; she read the cards and the tea leaves, and later on in life, she taught me the same skills.

From a young age, I always knew there was something different about me; having two psychic grandmothers living on opposite sides of the world, this is where I possibly inherited their gifts. Through the years, I would predict certain things for family and friends, and then in my thirties, I decided to take the next step and read Tarot professionally. Later, I was asked to write books for a few publishers, so my career was born.

Leanna, my only child, was very difficult to rear. At the age of three, she started to hear voices in her head, and it did cross my mind she might have a mental health condition. I spoke to my grandmother, who said bluntly, "She's not mad; it's obvious the child has a mediumistic gift!" I was bewildered; how could I keep this little girl safe? How could I help her control these voices? Fifty years ago, anything supernatural was still a bit of a taboo subject, and there was no internet to point you in the right direction.

As she grew, she witnessed orbs, incessant whispering, constant voices getting louder and, at times, more sinister. She also saw interdimensional beings such as fairies and other elementals. In those days, I didn't have a vast knowledge of supernatural matters; I taught her the Lord's Prayer, even though we weren't religious, which would calm things down for a while. One day when she was fifteen, she was in a huge shopping mall, and the voices intensified in her head to such an extent she ran through the crowd with her hands over her ears, screaming at them to leave her alone. Then suddenly, as if by magic, they disappeared, and she was never bothered by them again. I believed that as she grew older, her mind power became stronger, and she had somehow closed a door to these intrusive attacks but still managed to maintain her psychic abilities. When she was in her twenties, she, too, became a professional psychic, and as the years followed, we both went on to teach Tarot, palmistry, and Leanna, Wicca. Her writing career flourished, and she has penned more than a dozen books, and I can only say how proud of her I am. She was a remarkable little girl, and she's now so unique that I feel privileged that I was chosen to guide her.

—Beleta